THE SALLIE HOUSE:
EXPOSING THE BEAST WITHIN

THE SALLIE HOUSE: EXPOSING THE BEAST WITHIN

RENÉE PAWLISH

AND

JOE CETRONE

Llama Press Books
Colorado

A Llama Press Book

Llama Press
9576 West Walker Place
Littleton, CO 80123

ISBN (978-0-9827056-0-5)

First Edition: March 2010

0 9 8 7 6 5 4 3 2 1

Dedicated to

Joseph F. Cetrone
January 2, 1941 – July 12, 2005

Acknowledgements

Renée would like to thank: my parents, always supportive; also Joe Cetrone, Harl Hargett, Steve Gladen, Mark Klein, Stewart Robotham, Michelle Pawlish, and Jenn Velie.

Joe would like to thank: my wife Debbie for all her support; also Renée Pawlish, Joe Bodman a.k.a. 'the Onion', Pastor Wayne Fitzpatrick, and Dwayne Claud; and mostly my Lord and Savior, Jesus.

We both would like to thank: all those who shared so openly their experiences with the Sallie House: Deb and Tony Pickman, Todd Bates, Michael Piccerelli, Dawn Pierce, Mark Brown and Dan Hernandez. Without each of you, this book would not be what it is; Beth Hecker for her friendship and insightful advice; Beth Treat for her extraordinary editing; and Angie Eron and Barry Hall for their feedback on early drafts.

If we have missed anyone, please know it was not intentional.

Any omissions or mistakes in the book are solely those of the authors.

THE SALLIE HOUSE:
EXPOSING THE BEAST WITHIN

DRAMATIS PERSONAE

Joe Cetrone
Former investigator with Ocean State Paranormal Society (OSPS) and co-founder of Rhode Island Demonic Disturbance Investigative Association (RIDDIA). Co-hosted *Strange Encounters* and *Phenomenon/Strange Encounters* on WCAN Radio in Elyria, Ohio. Joe is also the author of two books, The Invisible War and God, the Bible, and the Afterlife, and a teacher on spiritual warfare and paranormal phenomena.

Michael Piccerelli
Former investigator with Ocean State Paranormal Society (OSPS) and co-founder of Rhode Island Demonic Disturbance Investigative Association (RIDDIA). Co-hosted *Strange Encounters* and *Phenomenon/Strange Encounters* on WCAN Radio with Joe Cetrone.

Mark Brown
Former member of the U.S. Army Reserves and currently a correctional officer for the State of Rhode Island. Mark, a member of RIDDIA, is interested in investigation of the spirit world from a Biblical perspective.

Brad Stafford
Producer of the Sallie House documentary.

Samantha Clay
Marketing agent and co-producer of the Sallie House documentary.

Dan Hernandez
Psychic from San Diego, California, with experience in assisting law enforcement officers to find missing persons and clues to cold-cases files. Dan also works with individuals to help them achieve closure with lost loved ones.

DRAMATIS PERSONAE

Anna Burrows
Member of Midwest Paranormal Research Society (MPRS).

Dawn Pierce
Former member of Ocean State Paranormal Society (OSPS) before joining Rhode Island Demonic Disturbance Investigative Association (RIDDIA), Dawn served as publicity agent for the radio show *Strange Encounters*. She also hosted her own radio show on WCAN called *Paranormal Encounters on the Other Side*. Her house was the subject of Joe Cetrone's first investigation.

Todd Bates
Highly respected paranormal investigator and Electronic Voice Phenomena expert from Palestine, Illinois. Todd is also the founder of *Haunted Voices Radio Network* in Chicago, Illinois, and was one of the first investigators of the Sallie House.

GLOSSARY OF TERMS:

Cold Spot: A significant drop in temperature in a particular place in a room. In a case of a haunting, a cold spot can be an indicator of an unexplained presence. Cold spots or other unexplained fluctuations in temperature are usually measured by a digital thermometer. Paranormal researchers believe that a cold spot is a result of a spirit pulling the energy from our earthly realm.

Electronic Voice Phenomena (EVP): Electronically generated and electronically discernable noises that resemble speech, but are not the result of intentional voice recordings or renderings. Common sources include static, stray radio transmissions, and background noise. Sometimes, there is no apparent source for these phenomena and some people believe that they are of paranormal origin. It is believed that a spirit can leave a voice imprint on a digital or analog recorder. In these cases, a person will not hear the voice audibly at the time of the recording, but once played back, a voice of unknown origin can be heard.

Active EVP Recording: Asking a spirit a direct question while investigators record the response with a digital or analog recorder.

Passive EVP Recording: Running an audio recorder for an extended period without any vocal communication with a spirit.

EMF Meter (or EMF Detector): An instrument that measures electromagnetic radiation fluctuations density (DC fields) or the change in an electromagnetic field (AC fields). It is believed that an EMF meter can detect a spirit's magnetic energy by measuring the magnitude and direction of a magnetic field.

GLOSSARY OF TERMS:

Orb: Sphere-like forms of energy of an unknown origin. Rarely seen with the naked eye, orbs can sometimes be viewed in photographs or with night-vision equipment. Some orbs appear transparent and dull-looking, while others are large and bright. In most cases, there are natural explanations for these objects (an insect, dust, or rain drops). Orbs usually appear in homes near lights, TVs, electrical outlets and computers. Authentic spirit orbs sometimes exhibit facial features such as eyes, nose, and cheeks.

Paranormal Investigator: One who researches the spirit world and gathers information to authenticate paranormal phenomenon. Some popular areas of paranormal studies include spirit hauntings, haunted houses, the occult, cryptozoology, the study of Bigfoot, and UFOs.

Psychic: A person who professes to have paranormal powers, or claims an ability to perceive information hidden from the normal senses through extrasensory perception (ESP).

Sensitive: A person who is susceptible to psychic influences. This individual may have "psychic" powers, but is not a medium, and does not possess the ability to communicate with the dead.

PROLOGUE

"Joe Cetrone, I never expected to hear from you again."

"Hello, Dawn," Joe replied. "How have you been?"

"I haven't heard from you since right after the investigation," Dawn Pierce said, sadness and hurt in her voice.

"I know. I'm sorry about that."

"You go to Kansas to investigate a house with paranormal activity, and when you come back, it's like you dropped off the face of the earth." Dawn sighed. "What happened?"

A long pause ensued as Joe stared at the ceiling, thinking back. What *did* happen?

Joe and his paranormal investigative team, Rhode Island Demonic Disturbance Investigative Association, had gone to Atchison, Kansas, to investigate the Sallie House. Scenes from that weekend played in his mind. The investigation had been an adventure and he'd had fun. The team had filmed everything for a documentary that they hoped would catapult them onto television. But he wondered about that. Had they done the right thing in filming the investigation? Since that time, in the back of his mind, Joe believed the Holy Spirit confirmed that God would not honor what they did because they lost sight of their original vision, which was to expose demonic activity in the house. Over time Joe came to believe that he had had no business going to the Sallie House in the

1

first place because, truth be told, their adventure was more for profit and gain than anything else.

And what about being in the house? Did any dark spirit attach itself to members of the team? And then there was Michael Piccerelli, Joe's investigative partner. He'd brought back dirt from the basement of the house, and toys from one of the bedrooms. Did that open them up to dark influences? Looking at what happened to Joe and others involved in the Sallie House investigation, it seemed like that could be the case.

Joe rubbed his eyes and frowned. "Dawn, the sad part is, right after we returned from the Sallie House, even before we started looking at the footage and bringing the documentary to life, I knew it was already over."

"What do you mean?" Dawn asked.

"It's like this," Joe began.

CHAPTER ONE

A year before, on a wintry night in January 2006, a blue Chevy Malibu sped through the Connecticut countryside, headlights piercing the darkness. Joe's lean, muscular arms clutched the steering wheel, his mind on what he was about to do. In the car with him were Michael Piccerelli and Ken Thompson, team leader of the group, and his wife, Sarah. They comprised Ocean State Paranormal Society, a team that conducted paranormal investigations. They were headed to a house in Woodbury, Connecticut. The owner, Andrea Smith, worried that her home might be haunted.

"This place is way out here," Joe said, noting that it had been a two-hour drive through dense forest from his house in Warwick, Rhode Island, to Woodbury. The night was blustery cold, ten to fifteen degrees above zero, and a full moon shone brilliantly in a sky speckled with bright stars. They soon arrived in Woodbury, a quaint town of around ten thousand people. Old houses sat well back from the main road with long dirt driveways bathed in shadows. Joe drove along dim streets with few streetlights and soon came to a newer suburb. He turned up a hill and around a bend to a white ranch-style house. He parked the car and everyone piled out.

Ken was a short, stocky man, nearing fifty, with the beginnings of a gut protruding over his belt. He ran a hand over his short brown hair and

3

a cautious smile split his baby face.

"Let's get started," he said slowly, as was his habit. He was a humble man, liked by everyone.

They unloaded their investigative equipment from the car and followed Ken into the house, where he introduced them to Andrea.

"I think there could be demons in the home," Andrea said with an edge in her voice.

"What makes you think so?" Ken asked.

"I was involved in Satanism years ago, and I think that the coven I was with might come back and hurt me or my family."

Andrea knew Joe was a Christian, and she wondered if he would preach to her, but he chose not to. This was Joe's first paranormal investigation, and his main purpose in being in her home was to sit back and observe the others. As he watched Ken and Michael set up video cameras, Joe reflected on how a thirty-four year old Italian ex-con with a high school education and a background that included Roman Catholicism, Satanism, and the occult came to join a paranormal investigative team.

+   +   +

Joe had always enjoyed horror movies and stories, and anything that had to do with the afterlife mesmerized him. But one key experience catapulted him into the realm of the paranormal. That defining moment occurred the previous July, when his father passed away.

Two days before his father's death, Joe sat on the porch of his home in Warwick, Rhode Island, with his godparents and his dad. They chatted pleasantly, enjoying the warm, sunny day. Then the topic of conversation abruptly turned to the Bible and the afterlife.

"Where do you think we go when we die?" Joe Sr. asked.

"We go to heaven," Joe responded, then elaborated on the Biblical vision of heaven and hell.

His dad nodded. "I believe, my son, and when God is ready to take me, I'm ready. He's been very good to me."

Two days later Joe Sr. passed away. Joe hadn't seen his father again

4

after that conversation. But Joe wondered about their talk. Did Joe Sr. know he was going to die soon?

After the funeral, Joe was at the family home, where he lived in the basement with his kids since his divorce two years ago. As Joe walked into the living room, he noticed a wind-up clock that sat on the mantel. It had a round, glass door covering the clock face and had been his father's favorite clock.

Lillian, Joe's godmother and good friend of Joe Sr.'s, was sitting in the living room with Joe's aunts and uncles and Joe's mother, Gloria, discussing the funeral and sharing memories of Joe Sr. Gloria noticed that the clock had stopped. She stood up, opened the glass door of the clock, wound it, then closed the door tightly with a 'click'. As she sat back down, the glass door of the clock swung open by itself. Lillian burst into tears.

"I know that Joe Sr. is here." She dabbed at her eyes. "He's telling me he's here."

They all began chattering about the clock.

"What's going on?" Joe asked as he came into the room.

"The clock," Lillian said, telling him what just happened. Tears rolled down her cheeks. "Your dad is telling us that everything is going to be okay."

They couldn't explain how the clock door opened since the door locked into place, nor could anyone explain how a week later the doorbell rang when no one was around. It didn't appear to be kids pulling a prank or faulty wiring.

Those incidents simmered in Joe's mind. Then, a couple of weeks after the funeral, *Ghost Hunters* aired an episode that took place in Rhode Island, and the show propelled Joe down the path of paranormal investigations. The show explained that heightened paranormal activity often occurs near cemeteries. Whether because spirits are roaming the earth or something else, no one knows these answers.

Joe had always wondered about his own house being haunted. Growing up, he and his mother periodically would hear heavy footsteps on the roof that echoed throughout the house, even causing the light fixtures to shake. They also sometimes heard the sound of a hammer pounding metal in the attic, but of course no one was there. But the television show made Joe speculate about his neighborhood as well. All the houses in the area were built in 1976. At that time, cemeteries and forest surrounded the land, and the housing development was built right in the midst of numerous cemeteries that dated back to the mid-1800s.

"Was it possible that the cemeteries were now cursed because houses were built on it?" Joe questioned. And what about his dad's clock door opening, and the unexplained sounds he'd heard growing up? Could it be that his house was haunted?

He pondered something else as well. According to the show, if several negative events occur in close proximity, it can be an indicator of paranormal activity. What about Joe's own neighborhood? It seemed that almost everyone had had something bad happen to them. A baby died of Sudden Infant Death Syndrome in one of the homes. Other neighbors suffered with cancer. And finally, some neighbors were involved at one time or another with Satanism. And Joe himself, years ago, had dabbled in Satanism and the occult, and used Ouija boards. Although these events occurred over a number of years, Joe noticed the pattern of negative incidents. What did all of this mean, if anything?

His curiosity building, Joe contacted The Atlantic Paranormal Society, from Warwick, Rhode Island, Lisa Ericson in turn called Curt and Ken Thompson, local demonologists. On a Saturday night in late September, 2005, Ken and his team came out to Joe's house. Ken Thompson, his wife Sarah, and Michael Piccerelli interviewed Joe and his mother, Gloria, set up audio recorders, took pictures, and videotaped throughout the house.

And something weird happened.

It was close to midnight. Marge, a friend of Joe's sister, was staying at the house, watching TV upstairs. Being hearing-impaired, Marge knew nothing of the investigators' visit in the home. As she lay on the bed watching TV, she saw two figures appear. They were grayish and transparent, without faces, hands, or feet. Marge watched as they seemed to "walk" in front of the TV, elevated a few feet in the air. She was so scared she hid under the blankets until they disappeared.

After Ken and his team left, Marge related this incident to Joe. He was shocked. "She knew nothing about the investigation, but saw those entities right during the middle of it."

Joe called Ken the next day and told him about Marge's experience. The incident did not impress Ken, for he had seen a lot of spirit activity. However, Ken was intrigued that Marge had described the spirits as being without faces, hands, or feet. He wondered if she'd seen a demonic entity, because in most photographic images of demonic spirits, the spirit appears with some limbs missing.

Ken and Michael returned to Joe's home the following week with their results. They had not caught anything on video, but they did record an Electronic Voice Phenomena, or EVP, a spiritual imprint on the audio recorder, that sounded like something breathing. Ken didn't think it could be human because they captured the EVP in an empty room. They also had a picture of a very bright orb, a sphere-like object unseen with the naked eye, but that showed up in photographs taken in the backyard. The orb had a thick outer core like a ring that looked almost like the moon.

Ken also said that OSPS researched the whole area to see if there were other indicators of possible paranormal activity, and Michael pointed out all the original cemetery sites were. He had even printed out maps that showed Joe's neighborhood and the exact locations of the cemeteries before the housing development was built. This piqued Joe's interest because Michael had listened to Joe's earlier description about cemeteries in the neighborhood. Michael had done his homework. Essentially, OSPS turned up little paranormal activity, but Joe was, nevertheless, hooked.

To say "thank you", Joe and his fiancée Deb took Ken and Sarah out to dinner. At that time Ken asked Joe if he wanted to join OSPS. Joe jumped at the opportunity. He went to meetings held at a local library, where the group discussed prior investigations, viewed videos, and brainstormed how to raise money to buy needed equipment.

Then finally, they asked Joe to accompany them on an investigation.

"I was so excited, and a little nervous. I didn't know what to expect as we drove to Connecticut," said Joe.

+   +   +

"Will we discover any paranormal activity in this home in Woodbury, Connecticut?" Joe wondered as he watched Ken place a video camera on a tripod in Andrea's living room.

"We'll finish setting up our equipment and see what we can find," Ken said. He proceeded to place another video camera in a bedroom.

Andrea then showed them around the house. Ken and Sarah walked around the house and snapped some photos. Andrea believed that some kind of paranormal activity was occurring in her son John's room, so Joe and Michael set up audio recorders in that room.

Joe had a miniature Panasonic tape recorder. He put the tape on a bureau, turned it on and left the room. A half hour later he went back to flip the tape over, but the recorder was shut off. He thought that the tape had run out, but when he checked it, it had shut off one minute into recording. He rewound the tape and played back that minute. He could hear when he left the room and shut the door. After that there were a couple of sounds, almost like fingernails clicking on the bureau, and one other noise.

Joe restarted the tape at the one-minute mark. He took some pictures around the house, then spent the rest of the time watching Ken interview Andrea. He didn't tell anyone about the tape until the end of the evening. They had ordered pizza and while they were eating, Joe rewound the tape and Michael heard the noise as well. Both thought sounded like a bark.

Later Joe listened to the EVP with headphones. Now he heard something different from a bark. It was a voice – loud, obnoxious, and evil. It sounded like it said, "Get out!" It blew Joe away. He played it for Ken, who heard it, too. They ran it through filtering software and cleaned up the audio, and could hear the EVP much clearer now. *"Get out!"*

"It was a mindblower," Joe says. "Man, was I excited about that. My first EVP, and it was something bizarre like that."

Ken did not find other indicators of paranormal activity in Andrea's home and, because he did not believe the EVP alone indicated true spirit presence, he did not follow up on the investigation. Even though Joe and Michael doubted Ken's conclusions, they did not share their assessment of the home with Andrea, because they thought Ken had resolved the case with her. Joe found out years later that Ken had not followed up with Andrea at all.

+   +   +

A month later, Joe went on his second investigation. Dawn and Mark Pierce lived in Everett, Massachusetts, just outside of Boston. She contacted OSPS after becoming increasingly concerned about her toddler's behavior.

Dawn first became aware of paranormal incidents when her seventeen-month-old son Jordyn would look toward the open basement door and say "Mama, ghost". This happened almost every day. At first she dismissed it as his overactive imagination. But then she began to feel as if someone was spying on her, even though no one else was in the room. She also heard her name being called a couple of times, and she felt something touch her on the back of her head. On more than one occasion, Dawn stuck pictures on a bathroom mirror, turned away momentarily, and when she looked at the mirror again, the pictures were hanging upside down. And as her son grew older, the activity he experienced increased. He did not want to play with toys in his bedroom, and Dawn and her husband frequently overheard him in the bedroom talking to someone or quarrelling over a toy.

When Jordyn was four, she heard him shout: "No, you tell them!" Another time, her husband heard Jordyn arguing, so he poked his head into the room. It looked like a toy was being tugged between two children, but Jordyn was the only one in the room.

9

Other residents in Dawn's apartment complex also complained of strange happenings. One neighbor reported cold spots (an area in a room with a significant drop in temperature, which can indicate an unexplained presence) in her apartment and strange noises in her attic. Another thought he saw an apparition that resembled a little boy in his apartment. None of the information was concrete, but it was enough to suggest the possibility of paranormal activity.

Joe found out later that the apartment complex had been built on cemetery grounds, that one of the neighbors read Tarot cards, and another practiced Wicca, but he didn't know that when he visited Dawn's house.

The OSPS team had visited the Pierces' house once and performed an initial investigation. They planned to drive there again at five o'clock on a Saturday in February, but Ken called Joe at nine that morning and backed out.

"It's supposed to snow," Ken said. "I don't want to drive there in a storm."

"How about Michael and I go?" Joe suggested. Since recording his first EVP, Joe couldn't wait to go on more investigations. He also felt a sense of urgency, since a child was experiencing the paranormal activity. (Many investigators, who believe that children are especially susceptible to the invisible realm because of their youth and innocence, want to help them quickly in order to alleviate their fright and potential nightmares and to prevent emotional damage or trauma.)

Ken hesitated, thinking of Joe's inexperience. However, since Ken had already worked with Dawn and her husband once before, he didn't see the harm in Joe going without him.

"I guess it wouldn't hurt for you two to go," he said.

Joe called Michael and told him the news, and later that night, the two set out for Everett. They bonded on the ninety-minute drive to Dawn's home, discovering that they had a lot in common. Both were from Catholic families, both love sports, and both were musicians. And they both wanted to approach paranormal investigations as Christians.

10

Dawn's apartment was similar to a typical townhome, four units to a building, with two bedrooms and a bathroom upstairs, a kitchen and living room on the main floor, and a finished basement. Once Joe and Michael introduced themselves to Dawn and Mark, Dawn described the paranormal activity in their home.

"I told them about Jordyn seeing ghosts in his room," Dawn says. "He described them as a family, and when he tried to draw them, they looked like triangles, apparitions with no legs. He even called them 'triangles' because they didn't really look human."

Dawn also told them about hearing noises in the attic, so Joe and Michael set up recorders in the attic and in Jordyn's bedroom. They took pictures, placed monitors around the house to check for cold spots, and talked with Dawn and Mark in the living room while the tapes rolled. In addition to Ken's investigative techniques, Joe and Michael prayed throughout the house.

They started in the attic. The attic door was nailed shut and Joe wondered if this was a sign that they should avoid the attic. But, he stayed silent, nervously shifting from foot to foot as Michael worked at prying the nails loose. Once the nails were out, Michael lowered the built-in stairs and climbed into the attic. Joe ascended the stairs and poked his head in. Michael's flashlight beam danced in the darkness, and Joe saw insulation and shadows. The air smelled stale and he shivered against the cold.

Joe took deep breaths to calm his fear, but he remained on the stairs, feeling safer there than in the attic. Michael said a short blessing, and Joe joined in from his perch.

"I couldn't wait to get that blessing done and shut the attic up and get out of there," Joe recalls.

They went to Jordyn's room and blessed it as well. They continued with blessings in each room, but when they got to the basement, Michael wanted to expand on what they were doing.

"Okay, Joseph," Michael said. "It's time to go to work."

Joe nodded enthusiastically.

The recorders rolled as Michael started to pray. He asked for protection for the family and for the house. Joe took out his Bible and read Luke 10:19: "Behold, I give you the authority to trample on serpents and scorpions, and over all the power of the enemy, and nothing shall by any means hurt you."

"This is a house of Christ. You are no longer welcome here, evil spirit," Michael continued. "And you know you have to obey our command to leave." He concluded his prayer and they stopped taping. Their examination was finished. They loaded all their equipment in the car, said goodbye to Dawn and Mark, and drove back to Rhode Island.

They talked the whole way home about the spiritual aspects of this investigation. What they had done in Dawn's house was unique because neither knew of any other paranormal investigative team that brought Christianity into its work. Joe and Michael wondered if they could branch out from OSPS and move forward as Christian investigators. A half hour before they arrived at Joe's house, flurries began.

The next day, Joe felt that his gut instinct to bring a Christian perspective to the investigations was validated. As he watched a Giants game on TV, he also played the audio recordings of the EVP. At first, he heard nothing but silence or Michael and himself talking, and, frankly, he was paying more attention to the football game than to the tape. At the end of the tape, he heard Michael pray, "You know you have to obey our command to leave." Just as Michael said "command", Joe heard an EVP. It sounded like an animal in pain, moaning deeply, and it sounded evil. His heart jolted. He was so surprised he flung the headphones away. For the first time since delving into paranormal investigations, he felt fear.

Joe kept listening to the tape, trying to convince himself the noise was something explainable. He decided to get another opinion so he sent the tape to Todd Bates, an EVP specialist in Illinois. Todd verified that, in his opinion, the EVP was genuine. He cleaned the recording up and then sent it on to a demonologist, who agreed that the EVP was definitely not that of a human spirit, whose EVPs differ dramatically from the animalistic sounds made by demonic spirits.

"From that point on, I followed my vision of going into homes as a Christian paranormal investigator," Joe says. "I would perform blessings and pray in the home, and invoke the name of Jesus. And Michael wanted to do the same thing."

CHAPTER TWO

Michael Piccerelli grew up in Barrington, Rhode Island, about a twenty-minute drive from Joe's house. From a traditional Italian family, he was a devout Roman Catholic. He was a handsome man, almost thirty years old, always well-dressed, and articulate. He was working as a car salesman when he became involved with OSPS.

Michael's journey to paranormal investigations differed greatly from Joe's. Michael wasn't enamored with ghosts and demons and the like. A year prior to joining OSPS, he wondered if he was battling a mischievous spirit in his home. While he slept, the clock, lamp, and things on his bureau, such as his wallet, would be moved elsewhere. These occurrences eventually convinced Michael that spirits may exist, but he wanted more proof. He immersed himself in gaining knowledge of the spirit world. He read voraciously, studying famous paranormal cases. The book, *Hostage to the Devil*, by Father Malachi Martin, was a favorite of Michael's. He learned about the variety of equipment used by investigators, and he memorized a number of prayers from the *Roman Ritual*, an official work of the Catholic Church. In essence, Michael was a researcher first, then an investigator. He became a believer in the paranormal after participating in investigations and documenting evidence of paranormal activity. And the more he immersed himself in the paranormal world, the more intrigued he became with paranormal phenomena. He even hoped one day to perform an exorcism, and considered entering the priesthood so he could help people who were demonically oppressed or possessed.

Fate seemed to play a hand in bringing Michael and Joe together. Not only were they both intrigued by the paranormal, both wanted to investigate cases that pertained to 'the demonic', or dark entities. Along with Joe's EVP from Dawn's home, Michael's tapes from her house included seven EVP's, one that clearly said, '*Pig*,' that he had recorded in the attic. The two had apparently stirred up malevolent spirits when they prayed in Dawn's home. It seemed clear to both men that their Christian approach had aroused these dark spirits. Now, could they help free people from these negative spirits?

Joe had for years been studying spiritual warfare, and was writing a book, *The Invisible War*, about the topic, when he joined OSPS and met Michael. Shortly after that, Pastor Wayne Fitzpatrick, who hosted the Internet radio show, *Phenomenon*, on WCAN Radio in Cleveland, asked Joe to be a guest on the show. *Phenomenon* explored a variety of topics related to paranormal activity and the invisible realm, and it had a time for call-in questions and answers.

Joe began to see a vision: Was God opening a door for Michael and himself to use radio to bring the message of Christ to people within the paranormal arena?

Michael and Joe took their idea to a local radio station, and soon they were hosting a weekly show, *Strange Encounters*, broadcasting on Sundays. Dawn Pierce joined them, serving as promotional director for the show. She also lined up guests: Other investigators such as Grant Wilson, one of the founders of TAPS (The Atlantic Paranormal Society), who had the hit television show *Ghost Hunters*; authors such as Rosemary Ellen Guiley, paranormal investigator and author of over forty books; and other experts in the paranormal field, such as Dwayne Claud, a demonologist; and Ryan Merritt, a renowned investigator. Their first guest was Todd Bates, the EVP specialist who had validated the EVP from Dawn's home. The show gained popularity and eventually merged with Pastor Wayne's show in Cleveland.

Bolstered by their success, Joe and Michael decided to form their own investigative team. They took their faith and beliefs, and decided to handle cases involving the 'demonic'. They wanted to help people who were plagued by dark disturbances by educating them from a Biblical standpoint about demons. They also wanted to study authentic cases of malevolent spirits from a Christian perspective, which was not the approach taken by secular investigators.

Their group, Rhode Island Demonic Disturbance Investigative Association, or RIDDIA, offered prayer, home blessings, and spiritual counseling while using scientific equipment to obtain evidence of demonic activity.

"When I think about it, we were a ministry 'flying under the radar' of the paranormal and secular worlds," Joe says. "It was a way to bring light into a very dark and empty world. I was familiar with that world because I lived in darkness with a void in my life for a long time. I had dabbled in the occult, playing with Ouija boards and Tarot cards as young as seven years old. By the time I was a teenager, I was praying to Satan, selling my soul to him, and reading Anton LaVey's *Satanic Bible*. When I was nineteen, I focused on my music and I walked away from Satanism. At that point, I didn't believe in anything. But five years later, I met a man who shared his Christian faith with me and a week later, after talking with him further, I became a Christian. I've felt such peace since that time and I've wanted to share it with others who experienced that same emptiness. Our team didn't use divination or try to communicate with the dead. We would simply run audio recorders while praying with the homeowners, take pictures where paranormal activity occurred, use digital thermometers to detect cold spots, and use video cameras to capture orbs or objects moving. If a client didn't want prayer or a Gospel message, we respected their requests, and only offered any evidence we'd obtained to validate the case."

Within a month of RIDDIA's formation, Mark Brown, a fortyish African-American, joined the team. Joe and Mark were pals, so close that Mark was the best man at Joe's wedding. Mark had been in the military and worked as a correctional officer. He was solidly built, strong, and he liked to wear a black leather jacket and dark shades, like a Hollywood 'tough guy'. He had no interest in the paranormal until Joe shared his vision of incorporating Christianity into the science of investigating the supernatural. Even then, Mark didn't want to get involved. He thought Joe was crazy, advising him to be careful, and not to get involved in divination. Joe told Mark how he wanted to go into houses where possible paranormal activity existed, listen to the stories of the person living in the home, pray with that person, and see if RIDDIA could obtain tangible proof of spirits, especially dark spirits.

Mark still didn't plan to get involved in RIDDIA. But then Joe let him hear the EVP of a demon's voice. The EVP frightened Mark, but also intrigued him. At that point, he decided to work with Joe and Michael's team. He saw a way of evangelizing to people who were dealing with paranormal activity.

"Mark is a spiritual bulldog," Joe says. "He's got a great heart for God, but he can be a little intense when you meet him. He'll preach the Gospel message to anyone, no matter where he is. He's a prayer warrior and someone who's great to have on the team."

The more Mark accompanied RIDDIA on investigations, though, the more he felt spirits were haunting him. He repeatedly told Joe he heard something walking on his bed. It scared him so much he couldn't sleep, and he sometimes called Joe in the middle of the night. Joe wondered if Mark was paranoid, but finally Michael and Joe agreed to investigate Mark's home. They set up audio and video recorders and performed the same blessing as they had done at Dawn's house. At the same point in the blessing where Michael used the Lord's name, they heard a demonic growl. When Mark heard the recording later, his eyes widened and he threw his hand over his mouth. He wondered how and when this spirit had come into his home – was it this spirit that caused division between him and his wife and that eventually caused his divorce? Prior residents in the home had divorced as well. Was there something behind this? Mark couldn't answer that question, but he still wanted to get help and to assist the team.

If someone contacted RIDDIA for assistance, Joe would use a series of interview questions to determine the level of paranormal activity in the home. Michael would visit the home and ask another series of questions and evaluate whether there seemed to be authentic demonic activity. After that, Joe and Michael would discuss their findings. If the activity appeared valid, they would investigate the home. And if the interview questions revealed malevolent activity, Joe and Michael would have Mark go with them on those investigations, using his prayer for protection.

"Joe and I dealt with paranormal cases of a very dark and terrifying nature," Michael says. "Cases known as demonic or with inhuman phenomena. In cases like this, people were being oppressed, attacked, and they're usually at their wit's end by the time we got involved. We fought this evil intelligence with faith and prayer. Most cases ended by us performing a blessing, and in the worst instances Joe would pray while Michael read from the *Roman Ritual*.

RIDDIA became well-known as the Christian Investigators or the 'Navy Seals' of the paranormal world because they took the cases most teams wouldn't, ones with dark hauntings and possible demonic manifestations.

"There are many stories of human spirits – ghosts, and proof of ghosts' existence," Joe says. "But where is the existence of God from a scientific point? I thought that if I can prove the existence of a demon by it responding violently to the name of Jesus Christ, wouldn't that authenticate the existence of God, since He created angels? In this way, Michael and I hoped the evidence we gathered would prove demons were real."

Meanwhile, they continued broadcasting *Strange Encounters*. Through the show, Joe and Michael became friends with Todd Bates, who told them about the Sallie House in Atchison, Kansas. "The Sallie House is a notorious haunt that people in the paranormal world are familiar with," Michael says.

The Sallie House had intrigued Todd ever since he had participated in a major investigation of the site, and he immersed himself in researching the house. According to Todd, almost every investigator who entered the home became consumed by it. They would feel a need to be in the home, and a desire to investigate it. And once they'd spent time in the home, they seemed affected by it. Many suffered from nightmares, some became emotionally distraught afterword, or they lived in fear. Some won't talk about what they've seen in the house, and more than a few have given up paranormal investigating after they've been in the home. Todd also believed that the spirits in the home would conform themselves to whatever the investigator believed them to be – if the investigator believed the spirit was human and not dangerous, then that's the way the spirit would manifest itself. And if one felt the spirit wasn't friendly, then the spirit wouldn't be. And finally, Todd told Joe and Michael how Tony and Deb Pickman, who rented the house for a couple of years in the mid-nineties, didn't feel that their experiences of activity in the home had been accurately portrayed on previous television documentaries.

Tales of the Sallie House amazed Joe and Michael. After listening to everything Todd said, it seemed to Joe that the media were afraid to say that the hauntings in the Sallie House might be demonic.

Todd believed that if anyone could go into the home and find out what was really occurring, RIDDIA would be the team that could do it. And he felt that they would be the ones to prove that the home suffered from demonic activity.

Joe and Michael decided to see if RIDDIA could investigate the house from their uniquely Christian perspective. They wanted to go to Kansas, interview the Pickmans in person, and collect scientific evidence of paranormal activity. They also wanted to pray in the home. And just maybe they would find evidence of demonic activity.

So Michael, on behalf of RIDDIA, emailed Deb and Tony Pickman, who still lived in Atchison. Deb and Tony had been the first residents of the Sallie House to report paranormal activity. They had heard unexplained noises in the house, and stuffed animals had been moved from where they had been. Then, unknown forces had begun to attack Tony. These attacks had intensified over time.

The Pickmans had grown weary of teams visiting the home to capitalize on their experiences, and they were understandably wary of RIDDIA. Michael explained that he wanted not only to conduct an investigation, but also to allow the Pickmans to tell their story accurately. He offered to have them on the radio show. The Pickmans remained cautious, but eventually agreed to be involved.

At the same time, Joe talked to the owner of the Sallie House, explaining that RIDDIA wanted exclusive access to the home for an investigation. The owner hesitated at first, but within a week he called Joe and agreed. The owner arranged to have the house open and the electricity and heat turned on in time for the team's arrival.

Once Michael learned that RIDDIA would be able to investigate the Sallie House, he posed some questions to Joe: What would happen if we go into this home and find demonic activity? And further, what if we are able to film an exorcism so others could see it? They began to imagine the possibilities: Michael saw fame and money, Joe saw the opportunity to speak of the existence of God to a large audience. They found a television producer who would fund the investigation.

And so, a simple trip to a haunted house in Kansas turned into a plan to film the pilot episode of a new television show about Christian paranormal investigators. And, in the process their goals to validate a demonic presence in the Sallie House, to help the Pickmans, became compromised by their actions.

CHAPTER THREE

An air of mystery surrounds the naming of the Sallie House. One story says that in the 1870's, a doctor owned the house, using the main floor for his practice. One night, a little girl named Sallie was brought to the house by her mother. The girl was suffering from severe abdominal pain, and the doctor diagnosed a ruptured appendix that required immediate surgery. As the tale goes, the doctor did not let the anesthesia take full effect, and Sallie awoke when he began the operation. She screamed in pain and struggled with the doctor, and then, just before she died, she gazed at the doctor with loathing in her eyes. Her spirit is said to have remained in the house. In another version of the story, Sallie herself lived in the house, rather than the doctor. However, no one has proof of a girl named Sallie ever living in Atchison. Some investigators believe a 'Sally' once lived in the house, but she was much older than the young child claimed to haunt the home. To further complicate the matter, Dan Hernandez, a psychic who assisted the RIDDIA team during its investigation, sensed an altogether different circumstance surrounding the death of the little girl, Sallie, which he shared with the team as he guided them through the house.[*]

---

[*] See page 54 for Dan Hernandez's psychic impressions about "Sallie".

Whatever the truth, there appears to be a significant amount of activity there, enough to attract television shows that delve into the paranormal happenings in the house. The challenge for Joe and Michael would be to convince someone to take another approach to the Sallie House story. That someone was Samantha Clay, a marketing agent from North Providence, Rhode Island, who had contacts with production companies. Joe had met Samantha at the local radio station that broadcast *Strange Encounters*, so he and Michael pitched their television show idea to her. When they initially met with her about the Sallie House in the fall of 2006, she was skeptical. Television already had shows about paranormal investigators – what would make a show about RIDDIA different? Joe and Michael showed her pictures of orbs and they had her listen to the EVP of the demonic growl from Dawn Pierce's house. They inundated her with information about the Sallie House, the proposed site for the first episode. They explained how the show would follow RIDDIA, modern day exorcists, as they investigated cases of dark hauntings. Finally, after multiple meetings, Joe and Michael convinced her, and Samantha got in touch with producer Brad Stafford. Brad had worked on numerous projects in the entertainment industry, from soap operas to composing film soundtracks, and he was always on the lookout for a new and different project that could be profitable. Like Samantha, the idea of a show on modern-day exorcists grabbed his attention.

Joe and Michael spent five weeks working with Brad. They had weekly meetings where they educated him on how RIDDIA conducted investigations, emphasizing the Christian aspects that distinguished them from other investigators. Brad recorded test footage to see how filming looked with the lights out, and where the movie camera would need to be when Joe or Michael prayed. They showed Brad what they did in an investigation from start to finish, how they would perform a blessing if they suspected demonic infestation, and the specific prayers they intoned. During all this, Brad searched for ways to make their documentary different from others on television. He even suggested that Joe and Michael wear priests clothing while at the Sallie House, but they quickly vetoed that plan.

Brad also wrote a script and printed out cue cards for Joe and Michael to read. He wanted a powerful introduction, an intriguing welcome message telling viewers what the documentary hoped to accomplish.

"What about the rest of the show?" Joe asked. "Is it scripted out?"

"Just the introduction," Brad said. "After that, you and Michael can ad lib, and that way, it'll be more natural."

Brad had written a scene where Joe and Michael would point at the camera as if they held guns and say, "We are the supernatural gunslingers", but Joe and Michael hated that idea, so Brad dropped it from the script.

As the preparations continued, Michael focused on the documentary and the potential for a reality television show. Although he never wavered from his desire to help people, he also began to see the money to be made from a series. People would have the opportunity to see paranormal investigations from a new, fresh perspective, and that could mean a successful, popular show.

It was becoming clear to Joe that each person on the team had different motives for the investigation, and he struggled with that. He wanted to help people and continue RIDDIA's purpose, but he also knew that he couldn't afford to fly everyone to Kansas, so he kept his worries to himself.

Once Brad was prepared, Joe scheduled a weekend to visit the Sallie House. But one conflict after another kept the team from flying to Kansas: Samantha had out-of-town business meetings; Brad was committed to another film project; the holidays arrived. They couldn't seem to get everyone on the same page. At that time, Joe was playing drums in a band, and he would hire a drummer to fill in for him on a weekend because he thought he'd be in Kansas, and then they wouldn't go. Joe lost money every time this happened. He wondered sometimes if this was some kind of warning sign that RIDDIA shouldn't be going to the Sallie House. He prayed about the obstacles, but in looking back on it, he felt that he didn't really listen to God's direction. The more Michael talked about a TV show and the possibilities of quitting their jobs, the more that appealed to Joe, and he began to justify the trip, concluding that God wanted RIDDIA to enlighten the world about the demonic.

Joe kept in touch with the owner, who was keeping the home empty until RIDDIA could visit, not allowing other teams inside. But the delays were frustrating to the owner, so Joe worked out a deal to compensate him. Then everyone on the team agreed on a proposed weekend, and they finalized a date in mid-January.

Joe spoke with Michael, finally voicing his concerns that the investigation was moving in the wrong direction. It had become a television show and money, and he feared that God wouldn't honor what they were doing. Michael disagreed. "Joe, we'll be on the map, we'll make money and be able to quit our jobs. Don't worry about it." Once again, Joe rationalized his reservations and helped with final arrangements. In a concluding meeting, everyone from RIDDIA and the production crew agreed that the purpose of the trip and investigation would be to film as much paranormal activity as possible, and that RIDDIA would use their Christian focus to distinguish themselves from the average ghost hunters.

Joe then discovered that Brad had wanted a psychic to be involved in the investigation. So Brad had Michael contact Dan Hernandez. Michael had developed a relationship with Dan prior to the Sallie House project. Michael trusted Dan's 'second sight' abilities. Dan had done some preliminary research on the house a couple of weeks prior to the team's final meeting, but he had never met Joe or Michael in person. Dan gave RIDDIA his insights about the Sallie House. He wrote a report on everything he sensed about the house before the investigation began and had the report notarized.

Dan mentioned in his written report that he sensed in the home a particular spirit who claimed to be 'Joanne'. She was not a protective spirit, but rather, Dan felt, an evil presence posing as a benign spirit.

Initially, Joe wasn't thrilled about using Dan in the investigation.

"We're shooting ourselves in the foot. We're losing sight of who we are and why we're doing what we're doing."

Joe was skeptical about using a psychic because it didn't seem to him like a Christian approach, and it wasn't how he envisioned RIDDIA's work. He wanted to be an instrument of God who helped people battling the kind of spiritual warfare that most other investigative teams either didn't think or care to do. But as he and Michael moved forward with the documentary idea, Joe found himself surrounded by non-Christians, and although he had no problem with this in general, he knew Brad and Samantha weren't approaching the investigation from a Christian standpoint. They wanted content for a good, entertaining show. As time went on, Samantha provided funding for the project and more people became involved, and Joe simply kept his mouth shut and went along, compromising his vision. He found himself, like Michael, getting caught up in Brad's ideas for the documentary.

A week before the scheduled trip, Tony and Deb Pickman joined Joe and Michael on the *Strange Encounters* radio show. They were engaging guests, discussing the bizarre things that had happened while they lived in the home, such as Tony being scratched and flung across the room, objects being moved from one place to another, and seeing full-bodied apparitions. They shared how the house affected other teams who spent time in the home: Some claimed something touched them; some felt nauseous; others experienced overwhelming fear; one investigator in particular became so scared of something he saw that he bolted from the house and never returned. Deb also shared how, as occurrences in the home became increasingly dangerous, she began to fear for Tony's safety.

After the show, Joe and Michael reiterated that the Pickmans could tell their story their own way, and Tony and Deb relaxed a little. As the date approached for RIDDIA's trip to Kansas, Tony grew excited about RIDDIA coming to the Sallie House, especially since RIDDIA was a Christian team. Deb however, remained reserved.

Michael believed that RIDDIA would obtain scientific evidence of demons by the time they left Kansas. Joe wasn't so sure. And Mark, used solely on investigations that involved malevolent activity, hesitated to go. But he saw himself as Joe's protector, so his attitude was, "I don't think we should do this, but if Joe is going, I won't let him enter that house without me."

Joe, Michael, and Mark spent the remaining days preparing for the trip. They had prayer groups pray for them. The three team members fasted, prayed incessantly, and read their Bibles. Joe asked Dawn Pierce and Todd Bates to send out emails to their contacts in the paranormal world to let them know about the investigation, and to solicit prayers and encouragement. Joe and Michael checked all their video cameras, tape recorders, EMF detectors, flashlights, and digital thermometers, and bought a huge supply of batteries (spirits will draw energy from the batteries so they don't last as long). As the preparations continued, their anxiety mounted.

One thought continually raced through Joe's mind: how is that 'thing' in the Sallie House going to receive them, especially if it is demonic and it knows that they are Christians? Joe worried that if the team went in unprepared physically and spiritually, they could get their butts kicked by whatever resided in the home.

It didn't help that others they invited to join them backed out.

Joe had approached Dwayne Claud, the demonologist, to accompany them. At first Dwayne seemed receptive, but he turned them down without saying why, other than he just felt it was best that he not go. Joe asked Pastor Wayne Fitzpatrick to come along, figuring he would jump at the opportunity. Wayne initially said yes, but two days later he called to say he had been in and out of the hospital with knee problems and the doctor advised him not to fly.

Everyone seemed to have a last-minute excuse not to go, and Joe wondered what about the Sallie House seemed to cause fear for notable people in the paranormal world. It made him think he was crazy to go to the house. So he relied on Mark all the more, knowing that they needed someone with great spiritual focus to cover their backs.

In that final week before he left for Kansas, Joe kept looking for signs, anything that might be a warning that he shouldn't go or a word of wisdom from God verifying that RIDDIA was doing the right thing. This thinking consumed him to the point that he saw signs even when they weren't there. And as before, Joe let himself get caught up in possible fame and money, and he rationalized away his concerns.

Others were uneasy as well.

Michael had his own share of trepidation. "Joe, I know we're going into a fricking storm in that house," he said repeatedly. "We have no idea what we're getting involved in."

"Chill out. It's going to be okay," Joe replied. In the end, Joe and Michael put aside their doubts. RIDDIA and the production team of Brad and Samantha were scheduled to leave on Friday morning, January 19th, 2007.

They all were edgy the night before. Joe's emotions were up and down. One moment he was fine, and nothing bothered him. And then he would be anxious and nervous – and a little scared because he didn't know what to expect.

They planned to investigate the Sallie House, take pictures, record audio and video, interview the Pickmans, and pray for God's blessing on the home. The group had no intention to provoke any spirits or entities. There would be no divination, no séances, or other psychic work. They were merely a Christian team who would use the power of prayer in the house. Simple, but would it stay that way?

"It was weird how things happened," Joe says. "I watched a show on hauntings that aired every Thursday night. And guess what the topic was that particular Thursday? The Sallie House. Here I am watching this documentary on the house and the next day I'm going to be there. It was wild."

Joe couldn't sleep. He watched a horror movie on television, then lay awake in the dark, all the while pondering, "Is this the right thing to do? Is there something specific that God wants me to do?" He prayed ceaselessly for protection. And he worried about the unseen forces in the home. Would they somehow come back with him and do something terrible to his family?

Thoughts like those filled his whole night, along with watching the clock as it ticked away the hours.

DAY ONE

CHAPTER FOUR

Friday 6 AM

Joe awakened earlier than usual. His wife Deb acted as if it were a typical Friday, not one in which her husband was leaving to visit the most haunted house in America. But as she left for work, she did say that she would be praying for the team, and that she knew the trip and investigation would turn out fine.

Joe and his wife lived in the basement of his parents' house, and he saw his mother when he went upstairs for coffee.

"Are you excited or nervous?" Gloria asked as Joe poured himself coffee.

"Both," Joe said. "There's such an air of mystery around the Sallie House, I just don't know what to expect."

Thoughts of the unknown kept him on edge as he went back downstairs and watched the *Today* show, drinking coffee and trying to calm his nerves.

Michael was uneasy, too. When he arrived at Joe's house, Joe overheard him talking upstairs.

"I'm a nervous wreck," he told Joe's mother. "I hate flying."

That was news to Joe. And what a time to find that out, an hour before they would leave for the airport! He told Michael to calm down,

31

that Mark would be coming over, they would finalize some plans and pray before heading to the airport, and that everything would be okay.

Mark showed up and the three men talked for a few minutes. Mark grilled Joe and Michael. "Are you sure you're prepared for this? Are you spiritually ready to confront whatever's in that house?"

Joe and Michael assured Mark that they were ready, but the tension crackled like sparks between them. Then they abruptly stopped chattering, caught their breath, and focused.

"We can do this," Joe said. "Don't let fear come upon us now. If this thing is evil, it wants us nervous, so let's not give in to that."

They prayed together for protection and safety, and for discernment to detect anything evil in the house. They prayed that their hearts and motives would be pure, and that they would be presented an opportunity to minister to the Pickmans.

At ten-thirty, Joe's mom drove them all to the airport, where they met the film crew – Brad and Samantha. They all checked in for their flight and then lounged in the waiting area. Brad and Samantha sat together, talking about business. They were the skeptics, not believing that paranormal activity existed in the Sallie House. "They weren't the ones who were about to put their spiritual footing on the line," Joe thought as he watched them. "They had nothing to lose."

Joe read his Bible and listened to music on the flight to Kansas, trying to loosen up. Darkness had descended when the plane touched down in Kansas City. Brad's brother, Greg, met them at the airport. Greg was a police officer and paramedic who lived in Kansas City, and he joined the group as a security person and medical advisor in case the team encountered any issues while at the Sallie House. Since Greg was from the area, he served as their tour guide as well. They rented a van and were soon speeding through the hills and fields of western Missouri. The weather was freezing cold and snow was falling, and by this time, it was dark. Joe had no idea where they were, but he was glad the plane ride was over. All he wanted to do was get a bite to eat and get a second wind. They stopped at a restaurant for dinner, and then hit the road

32

again. An hour after leaving Kansas City, they drove into Atchison.

+   +   +

Located in northeastern Kansas on the bluffs of the Missouri River, Atchison was founded in 1854. One of the oldest industrial communities in Kansas, it was settled by a collection of men interested in ensuring that the population of the new Kansas Territory would be in favor of slavery. Named after Senator David Rice Atchison, himself a proponent of slavery, the town of Atchison soon became a major trade route for overland freighters. After the Civil War, manufacturing flourished, and flour mills, foundries, and furniture factories sprang up. Atchison was one of the first cities in Kansas to be connected to the East Coast by telegraph, and by the turn of the twentieth century, numerous railroads ran into the city.

At first glance, Atchison is like many small towns in America. It boasts magnificent Victorian homes, brick-paved streets, numerous businesses, a pedestrian mall, a Wal-Mart, and Benedictine College, a small, Catholic liberal arts college.

Atchison's claim to fame is that it's the birthplace of aviatrix Amelia Earhart. Each July, Atchison attracts thirty to fifty thousand people to the Amelia Earhart Festival. Along with the festival's craft fair, air show, and one of the largest fireworks displays in Kansas, visitors can visit the Amelia Earhart Birthplace Museum.

While all of this helps define Atchison, its recent notoriety in the 1997 book *Haunted Kansas*, by Lisa Hefner Heitz, has catapulted the town into the spotlight in the world of paranormal enthusiasts. Now Atchison is known not only as the birthplace of Amelia Earhart, but as one of the most haunted places in America. And the community has capitalized on this. Visitors can choose from a variety of 'haunted activities', from trolley or walking tours of local haunts, a tour of the cemetery, a ghostly dining experience, tarot card readings and psychic visits, and tours of private homes during 'haunted season'. And finally, those searching for the ultimate fright can pay to accompany paranormal investigators as they explore some of Atchison's most famous haunts, including the Sallie House.

+   +   +

After weeks of preparation, they were in Atchison. The group stayed at the Glick Mansion, a beautiful, old-fashioned house just across the street from the Sallie House, with its own history of paranormal activity.

The Glick Mansion was named for its builder and ninth governor of Kansas, George Washington Glick, a lawyer who moved to Atchison from Ohio in 1869. The Victorian mansion has been restored as a small Bed and Breakfast. And like so much of Atchison, the mansion has its share of alleged hauntings. A benevolent ghost is rumored to ramble throughout the house, causing unexplained noises. Some visitors claim to hear footsteps when no one is present, and doors mysteriously open and close.

Friday 7 PM

The group took a few minutes to check in and freshen up, and then they headed across the street to the Sallie House. A small house right on a main road, the Sallie House was not what Joe had expected.

North 2ⁿᵈ Street is a busy thoroughfare in Atchison. The Sallie House itself is a plain white wooden structure built in 1872, with a long front porch and brick pillars. A tall elm tree, stripped of leaves in the January cold, towers over it protectively.

Michael studied the house, and a heavy, oppressing wave of doom came over him. He knew right then that RIDDIA was going to have a fight on its hands with whatever had invaded the house.

The owner had unlocked the door and turned on the heat and electricity earlier in the evening, so everyone walked in and surveyed the inside. Because people were frequently in the house performing investigations, the electricity and water were on. A stairway led to a couple of upstairs bedrooms. To the right of the entry was a small living room. At the back of the house was a small kitchen with a doorway leading to the basement, and a bathroom. The only pieces of furniture

34

were a table and chairs in the living room. The atmosphere of the house was very warm and comfortable. Joe kept thinking, "How can this place be haunted?"

They had the house to themselves – no one had lived in the Sallie House for a couple of years. It was already after seven o'clock, and they knew they wouldn't be able to accomplish much, other than to get a feel for the home and film some trial footage. Samantha videotaped them with a camcorder. In preparation for Saturday's official filming of the documentary, Brad set up the movie camera and checked the angles and gave Joe and Michael some directions. Brad then tested the lighting in the house, had Joe read some sample cue cards, and took some pictures around the house. Brad worried the whole time that they wouldn't get enough recordings of paranormal activity to make a full-length feature.

At eight-thirty, Deb and Tony Pickman arrived. A down-to-earth couple, friendly and engaging, they were nevertheless cautious with the investigative team and camera crew. Deb, tall and blond with a warm smile, had a keen interest in the Sallie House, even though they hadn't lived there in more than ten years. As the camcorder rolled, but without the professional camera, microphones, or lighting, the Pickmans sat with Joe and Michael in the living room for a casual interview. Deb brought a laptop and showed them evidence of paranormal activity gathered in the home: Pictures of orbs; a picture of a shadow person in front of a door; and EVPs. Tony, rubbing his hand through his short, spiky blond hair, described how, when he lived in the house, he had been scratched, heard knocking or rapping in the walls, was touched or burned, heard disembodied voices, and was almost pushed down the stairs.

Then Deb and Tony gave the group a tour of the house, pointing out where they had experienced paranormal activity in each room. In the kitchen, an apparition had appeared in the window. In the kids' bedroom, toys had been moved. In the master bedroom, Tony had seen the door abruptly close, then something had flung him across the room.

The tour ended in the unfinished basement.

"It was pretty gross, like most basements are, dirty, dingy," Michael says. "Everybody was really afraid of that area of the house. Deb and Tony agreed to go down there, which was a big thing for them because they worried that Tony might be attacked down there."

As the group walked down the wooden staircase, their footsteps echoed, and they smelled the dank odor. Joe sucked in a breath as he entered the basement. He noticed the furnace, water heater, and exposed pipes running along the ceiling, but something else made him anxious. He spied splotchy black paint covering part of the cement floor, as if the paint were hiding something underneath. Todd had sent Joe photographs of a pentagram painted on the floor of the basement and explained that it was supposedly used as part of a protection spell. Outside the pentagram, someone had written 'Raziel' in orange letters. In Jewish mysticism, Raziel is an archangel, the 'Keeper of Secrets', but Joe didn't know the significance of it being used here. No one seemed to know either who painted the pentagram or the name Raziel, or who painted over the pentagram and name with black paint. As Joe stared at the black paint, apprehension washed over him. What kind of evil might they be dealing with?

Across the room, an opening led to a small crawlspace. Rocks, pebbles, and broken glass were strewn about. Some investigators believed a portal, or a 'vortex', as Todd called it, was in this area of the basement, which allowed spirits to enter into the earth's physical realm. When Joe spotted the crawlspace, goose bumps ran up his arms. Even though he knew about the portal, he was still spooked, not knowing if it was his imagination or some aura of the Sallie House itself.

A heavy silence blanketed the basement. Greg, the policeman, who stood next to Tony, looked around. He then turned back to Tony and said, "Man, your head's bleeding."

Everyone stared at three bloody scrapes that ran down Tony's forehead.

"It looks like a tiny pitchfork scratched him," Michael observed.

Tony had noticed a burning sensation on his forehead but did not realize he'd been scratched until Greg pointed it out to him. Tony later noted that he was accustomed to things like this happening, and had become numb to it.

They brought Tony upstairs. On the way up, Mark, already uncomfortable in the home, voiced his concerns to Joe. "Are we getting set up for something really bad?" he whispered. "We've got to know what we're doing or whatever is in this house will destroy us."

Back in the kitchen, they all examined the scratches. Greg, being the paramedic, tended Tony's wound and verified that it was fresh.

Michael and Mark followed Deb and Tony into the living room, but Joe stayed back with Brad and Samantha.

"What do you think?" Samantha asked. "Did he fake getting scratched?"

Brad shrugged. "I don't know. It's certainly possible."

"I agree," Joe said. "It happened really fast, but he still could've done that to himself."

Friday 9 PM

Once Tony's cuts had been cleaned, Joe and Michael asked him if he wanted to continue. Tony assured them he was fine, so everyone gathered in the living room. Joe, Michael, Deb and Tony again sat at the table, getting to know one another and discussing the house, while Samantha continued filming with the camcorder.

After a moment, Tony stood up. "What's that smell?" he asked. "It's a flower, or a woman's perfume."

Michael moved over by Tony and sniffed the air. "I smell it, too," he said.

"It's flowery, like lilacs," Joe said. The odor spread throughout the room.

"I feel something cold on my back," Tony said. "Do you see anything?"

He lifted up his shirt. A four-inch scratch mark ran down his back, red and bloody, as if a fingernail had cut across his skin. Samantha came closer with the camcorder. The group stared at Tony's back where a fresh wound appeared, shaking their heads.

As before, Greg verified that the latest scratch was new, while Joe and Michael took pictures of the wound and the room.

"We were all floored that this just happened," Joe recalled later. "I wondered again, could he have scratched himself? But Mark told me later that he'd been watching Tony closely, that Tony couldn't have inflicted the wounds himself. We went over the camera footage later, and Tony never left our sight. He never disappeared."

Tony's injuries shocked Brad, but also pleased him in a weird way, because now he had some sign of paranormal activity for the documentary. Joe and Michael now believed unequivocally they were dealing with a demonic haunting, because a benign spirit wouldn't harm someone.

Once the excitement of Tony second injury died down, Anna Perlman, a member of Midwest Paranormal Research Society (MPRS) arrived at the house. The MPRS team had investigated the house many times since Deb and Tony had moved out. Deb had asked Anna to visit during RIDDIA's investigation because Anna was familiar with the paranormal activity in the house. Once introductions had been made, Tony showed Anna the scratches on his back and head. Anna was taken aback, but had a decidedly different, more benign view of the activities in the Sallie House. She felt that Tony intimidated the spirit, so it wasn't attacking him so much as protecting itself. It also seemed to Joe that she might've been downplaying the incident by saying that a female spirit attacked Tony because it was somehow jealous of him, but she definitely did not believe it could be demonic.

MPRS had gathered extensive evidence from in the house, including pictures and EVPs that Anna offered to share with Joe and Michael. She also expressed her concerns about what Joe and Michael might do from a Christian standpoint – would they provoke the spirits by performing an exorcism? And would they attempt to rid the house of spirits?

Joe wondered if perhaps Anna didn't want the spirits exorcised because she spent time at the Sallie House almost every weekend.

"You seem to enjoy being here," Joe said to Anna. "The spirits don't scare you?"

"The house makes people feel peaceful," Anna replied. "The spirits aren't harmful. I know some of the individual spirits by their odor, and I've never felt threatened by any of them."

"It's like you know them and have bonded with them," Joe said.

"Yes." Anna nodded emphatically. "That's it exactly."

She also thought that different spirits frequently passed through the house and that the house was a "spiritual bus stop", a portal, for these spirits. But the spirits with which she was familiar were not vicious or mean.

"I've been in contact with a spirit named 'Joanne'. Supposedly she's Sallie's caretaker," Anna said. "She's never tried to harm me."

Joe did a double-take, because he remembered Dan Hernandez's report mentioning a spirit named "Joanne". "Dan was right on," Joe thought. He was fascinated because Dan and Anna had never spoken to each other.

Joe wondered as he listened to Anna if her beliefs about the spirits actually made the situation far worse, for a demon will use deception, its best weapon, in order to encourage humans to 'warm up' to it. This makes entities stronger, and he believed all the activity at the Sallie House was a direct result of such deceptions.

Joe and Michael enjoyed visiting with Anna and hearing more stories about paranormal activity in the Sallie House. Mark, however, being the spiritual bulldog, continued to voice concerns. In talking with Anna, Mark learned that her beliefs were of a pagan, Wiccan nature. He also saw that she wore a pentagram. This made Mark uncomfortable, but beyond that, he didn't agree with her views on the house.

"There's something suspect about her," he told Joe as the two chatted by themselves in the kitchen. "Anna's saying the spirits aren't threatening, but this thing just attacked Tony, so how can the spirits be benign? It doesn't make sense."

39

Joe listened, but didn't want to debate anyone's opinions of the house or their personal beliefs. He was more concerned with the investigation and the findings and conclusions they themselves would gather. He had no problem listening to Anna's theories and beliefs, knowing he didn't want to 'Bible bash' anyone with his beliefs. He simply wanted the opportunity to draw his own conclusions about the Sallie House. He knew the team had only seventy-two hours to do this, so he tried to have Mark focus on that.

Mark left the room and Joe stared out the window for a moment. He crossed his arms over his chest to quell the shaking that overtook him. During Tony's attacks, Joe was on an adrenaline high, but now that he was calmer, fear set in. He rubbed the sweat off his palms, and took some deep breaths. He feared that he or others might be in danger, and he worried that if the entities in the Sallie House were as powerful as they seemed to be, he might not make it home to his wife and children. He worried that in his desire to investigate the house, had he put the others in jeopardy. And he wondered if anyone else would believe what they were witnessing?

It was now close to one in the morning, the end of a very long day. Joe, Michael, Mark, Samantha, and Brad returned to their rooms at the Glick Mansion. However, Anna stayed overnight in the Sallie House. Greg, being a police officer, decided to stay at the house as well to guard their equipment and ensure that no one disturbed anything in the house in order to create a hoax.

Joe, Michael, and Mark shared a room at the Glick Mansion. All three were too wound up to fall asleep right away, so Joe put a movie, *The Descent*, into the DVD player. Joe still couldn't believe he was actually in Kansas, investigating the Sallie House. But he also had to deal with some animosity that was developing between Mark and Michael because of their different approaches to the investigation. Michael wanted to obtain scientific evidence, and he wanted to film an exorcism with verifiable results that RIDDIA could present to the world. And, unlike Mark, he didn't want to impose his Christian beliefs on the

Pickmans, Brad, and Samantha.

Michael irritated Mark, who voiced his concerns to Joe. Mark felt that Michael was acting like a know-it-all. "But if he knew it all," Mark said, "he would know that we're here to find out if what's in the house is evil and get it out, not to befriend anyone. Instead, you've got a witch in there!"

"I agree with both of you," Joe said. "I want to get scientific evidence and rid the house of any spirits, but I also want to share the Gospel with the Pickmans and educate them about the dangers in the house." He held up his hands. "Let's stay focused. We have a big day ahead of us."

"All right," Mark and Michael agreed.

Joe wondered, however, if his team and the production crew were splintering into separate camps with differing goals.

Later, when Joe turned out the lights, he lay on the bed and mentally ran through the day's events. He could sense by Mark and Michael's restlessness that they were doing the same. Fear rattled him. Whatever was in the Sallie House sure seemed pervasive and strong to them all.

Joe's last thought before he fell asleep was, "We're here. We made it, and we'll get a lot more accomplished tomorrow." He was excited because they had already obtained actual evidence with Tony's cuts. Now he could say it's not all in people's minds – the house is haunted. "Let's get some more evidence, but don't blow this. Let's do a good, quality show that we can sell, and we'll have a hit show and a way to educate people about the supernatural."

And just what would the Sallie House have in store for them in the morning?

DAY TWO

CHAPTER FOUR

Saturday morning

The team awoke early the next morning, ready for further filming of their investigation. Gray skies hung low overhead and the temperatures hovered in the teens.

Even though he had a lot on his mind, Joe enjoyed a wonderful breakfast at the Glick Mansion. The entire group sat at a big table and their hosts served a three-course meal. Joe settled in, feeling as if he lived in the mansion, instead of being just a guest.

After breakfast, the team and production crew ventured across the street to the Sallie House. They spent the remainder of the morning working on the show's introduction.

Snow was in the forecast for later in the day, but already the wind was blowing powder off the rooftops. Joe and Michael had a hard time pretending that they weren't freezing while Brad filmed them. In all the outside shots, the sound of their boots crunching over the snow could be heard.

Joe and Michael took turns introducing themselves, then Michael, reading from cue cards, introduced their show. "This is a show to educate, validate, and prove the authenticity of a house with paranormal activity." He was a natural in front of the camera, delivering his lines smoothly. He often completed a scene in one take.

Joe, on the other hand, had more trouble. He kept flubbing his lines. As his frustration grew, so did his mistakes. "I got through a whole scene and right at the end I said "supposedbly" instead of "supposedly", Joe said. "So I had to start all over again. And the more I had to repeat the lines, the more I screwed up the lines. I grew so aggravated at myself that I had to force myself not to swear at Brad." He also forgot to look into the camera as he spoke, so he would have to do the scene again.

"Don't stare at the cue cards for too long," Brad directed them. "Otherwise it will look like you're not gazing into the camera."

The longer they worked on the introduction, the colder they grew, and it became even harder to act as if they were not shivering as the camera rolled.

As they finally wrapped up the introduction, a reporter from the *Atchison Times* arrived. In such a small town, a new team investigating the Sallie House was interesting enough to make the paper. The reporter asked for Joe and Michael's assessment of the home, whether they thought it was haunted. Then the local television station's news team arrived. Joe and Michael took the TV news team on a brief tour of the house, and the reporter spent ten minutes interviewing them in the master bedroom.

Brad had been worried since the inception of the documentary idea that RIDDIA would not record enough paranormal activity to fill a show, so he decided that Joe and Michael should interview Anna, from MPRS, on camera. Brad had arranged to interview a local priest and rabbi for some religious perspectives on the happenings at the Sallie House, but neither showed up, so Anna's interview would present a different team's perspective. Anna explained that MPRS covered hauntings in Kansas. Their first big investigation, the Sallie House, occurred a several years after the Pickmans moved out. Since then, MPRS had been in the house numerous times, provoking responses from spirits while capturing EVPs and images of orbs. Anna reiterated her belief that the house was a spiritual "bus stop" and that she had never sensed that the spirits in the house were demonic.

After the interview, Brad had Greg, the security man and paramedic, step in front of the camera for an interview. Greg would serve as the 'rational skeptic', because although he didn't believe in the paranormal, he had witnessed Tony's injuries the night before. Brad thought it would be good to have Greg state for the camera that Tony's wounds were not fabricated.

As Brad and Samantha prepared for the next sequence of footage, Joe and Michael chatted with Anna about the spirits in the house. Anna thought that when the Pickmans lived in the home, the spirit named "Joanne" was protecting the Pickmans' baby. Anna played a couple of her recorded EVPs for Joe and Michael, and the EVPs sounded like that name. Anna felt that another spirit named "Polly" also occupied the home. She played a videotape from an investigation where a camera had been positioned to film the stairs. On the tape, Anna's voice called out, "Come here, Joanne, Polly," in a sing-song, friendly voice. As she spoke, two softball-sized spheres came up the stairwell. Then Anna spoke again. "Oh, you know I love you." It was as if she were acknowledging them and they were acknowledging her in return by coming up the stairs. It blew Joe away, but he also marveled at the level of activity in the house. Anna talked about the spirits as if they were children, as if they were living. And seeing the orbs respond to them, he could see why Anna liked being there, because she was constantly in touch with spirits.

Michael thought Anna was trying to sway their opinion of the house, saying, "Look guys, we know this house. It's not demonic – they're human spirits – it's like a family." "Demonic" was not in their vocabulary.

Saturday 11 AM

To help fill out the story for the documentary, Brad wanted to film footage around Atchison, so they packed up the camera equipment and drove to some other local haunts.

They stopped first at the Waggener House, otherwise known as the "Gargoyle Home", located a few blocks from the Sallie House. Built in the mid-1880's by B.P. Waggener, a lawyer and politician in Atchison, the impressive house is listed in the National Register of Historic Places. The house received its nickname from the two reddish-colored gargoyles that adorn its roof, said to have been placed there by Waggener as a symbol of his pact with the devil to make him wealthy. Legend says that an evil spirit troubled the house. A subsequent owner of the home who tried to remove the gargoyles fell to his death on a staircase in the home, and paranormal investigators have reported not only feeling a presence in the home, but also claimed to have detected evidence of spirits with their electronic equipment. Since the Gargoyle Home is privately owned, Joe and Michael only filmed a short segment in front of the house as they related its history.

"It was a great little town, somewhat 'tourist-y', with a focus on the paranormal," Joe recalls. "Generally, everyone that we talked to was friendly, and almost everyone we spoke with believed in ghosts."

Their final destination was the Visitors' Center, housed in the same building as the Chamber of Commerce and historical museum. Once the Santa Fe Depot, the restored structure is said to be haunted by the ghost of "Hangman Brad", a railroad worker who liked to hang from cargo as it was being loaded on and off train cars. He was killed when a cable carrying a load of cargo broke and he was buried beneath the load. Those who work in the building today report hearing the sound of footsteps above them, even though the depot has no second story.

The staff at the Visitors' Center did not have much to say. Joe told them about RIDDIA and their project, but the staff seemed cautious and reserved, as if they weren't allowed to talk about their views on the paranormal. Nor would they allow Brad to film and interview in the offices.

After lunch at the Sonic, they headed to the Pickman home, where they were to interview Deb and Tony in greater depth than the previous evening. Joe felt an added pressure because Brad had asked them to speak more distinctly and professionally than on Friday night. Because Joe knew the microphone was on and the camera was rolling, he froze a few times and fumbled his words. Finally, after a couple of takes, he began to relax in front of the camera.

The Pickmans grew less guarded as they shared more of their history with the house. Deb spoke again about how she and Tony were frustrated on many levels. She first expressed how their privacy had been invaded repeatedly with all the media hype surrounding them. They were also aggravated that the media stories twisted the truth of what happened to them while they lived in the Sallie House, especially the show *Sightings* and the movie *Heartland Ghost*, because those productions downplayed the paranormal incidents that had occurred to them.

Both discussed the emotional toll of dealing with the Sallie House. The whole experience had left them fearful, especially Tony, who worried that the entities in the home were actually trying to kill him. He also had vivid nightmares where he was killing Deb, and he believed it was the spirits influencing his mind. The final incident drove them from the home. Tony had been standing at the top of the stairwell. Just then he had an overwhelming sensation that he was about to be thrown down the stairs. That was when the Pickmans decided to move. And even though the Pickmans hadn't lived in the house for over ten years, they maintained a somewhat inexplicable curiosity about the house and its spirits. Deb and Tony became friends with the members of MPRS, and frequently visited the house during paranormal investigations. Deb and Tony also filmed interviews in the house for other television productions. And each time Tony went into the house, something attacked him. From what Deb and Tony described, it seemed to Joe as if the Pickmans couldn't break away from the negative influences of the house. Why else would they visit the house again? During and after the interview, Joe developed a real sense of compassion for them, and he realized that RIDDIA was called there to help the Pickmans rid themselves of the torment that held them.

Tony then showed everyone a picture on the shelf that he had drawn a few years before, his depiction of what the little girl Sallie might've looked like. It was so good that Brad eventually used it in the documentary trailer.

After the interviews, Brad decided they should take a break, so Joe, Michael, and the production crew left the Pickmans and went back to the Glick Mansion.

Saturday 3 PM

After resting for a bit and cleaning up, Joe went downstairs for a drink. As he headed back to his room, he passed by Samantha's open door. She had showered, dressed, and was sitting on the bed answering emails on her phone. Joe stopped and chatted with her.

"What do you think so far?" Joe asked her.

"It's been interesting, but I want more evidence," Samantha said, echoing Brad's concern. "If we can get more, we'll definitely have an informative show."

"We do have video of Tony getting scratched," Joe pointed out.

"And I'm happy with that. But we need to get weird things, like objects moving. The freakier, the better, in order to sell it."

"Well, we have the investigation later, so maybe we'll get something tonight," Joe said. He nodded his head. "What about this place? They say the Glick Mansion is haunted. Have you seen anything so far?"

"No, have you?" Samantha said.

"No," Joe replied.

Right then, a wet towel lying on the bureau lifted up into the air and dropped on the floor. They both looked at each other, astonished.

"Did you see that?" Samantha asked, awe in her voice.

"Yes, I did," Joe said. He was equally stunned, and he took it as a sign that they would obtain more evidence.

They examined the towel, looked around the bureau, and then

photographed the bureau and floor, hoping to capture a spirit entity. The towel was wet and heavy, impossible for a fan or the wind, even if either were present, to blow it off the bureau.

Joe yelled for Michael and Brad, and explained to them what had happened. They were all amazed. Brad and Michael wished they had witnessed it, and lamented that they hadn't been able to film it.

"We could've just been making up a story," Joe said later. "But we weren't. It really happened. And it made me believe it when people say the whole town is haunted!"

After that, everyone finished getting ready, and they all tramped back across the street, where the Pickmans and Anna from MPRS were meeting them. They would now conduct their investigation of the Sallie House.

CHAPTER FIVE

Saturday 4 PM

By now Joe and Michael were familiar with some of the things that happened to Deb and Tony in the Sallie House, so they had the Pickmans show them around, filming where some of the paranormal events occurred. This time, the Pickmans related more details as they went from room-to-room. In one of the bedrooms, Deb felt a cold spot.

"Right here," she said, waving her hand near the wall. "Don't even touch it, just graze your hand over the area."

Joe felt a surge of excitement, because he could feel not only the temperature drop but the energy where the cold area was, and he wondered if a spirit were following them through the house.

As the toured progressed, Mark was downstairs carrying on a heated discussion with Anna, arguing that the forces in the house were demonic, and asking her if she "knew Jesus". He was also praying and talking about God. As their voices grew louder, it began to interfere with the film audio.

Samantha pulled Joe aside. "He's going to blow the scene."

Brad expressed his frustration, too. "Joe, you have to do something about Mark. He's going nuts, talking religion, and he's making people uncomfortable. He's acting like a zealot, and I'm going to ask him to leave and go across the street if he can't subdue himself or if you can't get him to stop."

Joe agreed, and took Mark outside for a break, talking to him about what Brad wanted, explaining that Anna's beliefs were her beliefs, and that Brad couldn't get the shots with Mark railing in the background. "Please," Joe implored, "keep it down." Mark frowned and shook his head but kept his mouth shut after that.

While Joe talked to Mark, Brad shot a scene with Michael and Tony sitting midway down the staircase. Michael chatted a bit about the house, and asked Tony a few questions. Everything appeared absolutely normal. Michael found it remarkable that later, when everyone was back in Rhode Island and they played the tapes of that scene, they saw an orb of light dash in front of Tony and him.

The crew moved to the living room, ready for the introduction to the actual investigation. As the camera rolled, Michael read from a cue card, "We're in Day Two at the Sallie House, and we're going to start our investigation. We're going to phone Dan Hernandez, a psychic from California, and he's going to join us."

After filming the introduction, the group relocated to the master bedroom upstairs. Present were Anna, Michael, and Joe as investigators; the production crew of Brad and Samantha; and Deb and Tony.

With Samantha holding the microphone and Brad filming, Joe took his cell phone and a piece of paper with Dan's phone number written on it out of his pocket. He dialed the number and put Dan on speakerphone. Joe wanted to show that things were not rigged, that Dan was talking with them live, and it wasn't a pre-recorded conversation.

Joe spoke to Dan, "I would like to have you lead the way where you're feeling the most activity drawing to you."

Then they let Dan guide them.

"I'm sensing some energy in the master bedroom. Go in there," Dan said.

But once in the bedroom, he told them the spirit had moved into the smaller bedroom which had been the children's room when the Pickmans lived in the house. "I'm feeling the presence here," he said.

Michael paled as he walked into the room, as if he sensed a dark presence. Deb glanced around the room, concern etched on her face.

Dan mentioned this presence, and they felt the temperature drop.

"I'm sensing Sallie and her dad," Dan continued. "Sallie was a very sick little girl. She had an infection in her lungs. I see and feel her coughing and having problems breathing. The doctor who tended to her may have also been her dad. They feel like one and the same. He tried to operate on Sallie but killed her. Sallie also felt scared while living in the house, and she saw things that kids should not see or hear. She would often hide in the nursery in the corner by the window."

Then without explanation, Dan urged them all to pray. So Deb, Tony, Mark, Michael, and Joe stood in a circle and prayed the Lord's Prayer. Anna had agreed to stay out of the way during the investigation, so she stood outside the door watching. Joe didn't know why they began the Lord's Prayer, they all just spontaneously spoke it.

After the group's prayer, Dan said that the presence had faded from the room. And everyone noticed the temperature rise dramatically.

The entity seemed to be bouncing from room to room. Joe and Michael would detect some energy around them just as Dan would say he felt activity. As this continued, Joe thought, "Wow, what is going on here? Dan's never been in this house, and he's guiding us around where the spirits seem to be."

In each room, Joe and Michael took photos and recorded audio to capture EVPs. Large, bright orbs showed up in the digital photographs. And later, when they examined the images more closely, some of the orbs clearly showed eyes, nose, hair, and cheekbones. However, the audio recordings did not pick up any EVPs.

Dan's directions came so fast that Joe felt they were scrambling to document it all, and Brad was getting caught up in the excitement. Although Joe wanted to do more prayer, read Scriptures, and possibly exorcise the spirits, he also didn't want to interrupt Dan who seemed to be accurately tracking the spirit presence. So Joe kept his reservations to himself.

"The presence feels strongest in the basement," Dan said next.

Everyone rushed downstairs. The overhead light bulb barely illuminated the darkness, and shadows flickered on the walls. A loud click broke the silence as the furnace kicked on. They all jumped, then Joe chuckled. Deb exhaled loudly as she smiled uneasily. "That spooked me," she said.

Joe handed his cell phone to Brad and used his EMF detector used to try to identify spirit energy. As Joe and Michael stood near the black painted spot on the floor, Dan continued talking, "It feels to me like there was a ceremony or ritual that took place down there." Dan described how someone who lived in the house prior to the Pickmans drew the pentagram on the floor, thus opening a gateway for spirits into the house. He went on to say that when Deb and Tony moved in, the entity already resided there and attacked Tony because he was sensitive to the supernatural realm.

Joe, Michael, and Brad noticed a few dead wasps on the floor near the pentagram. In some known situations of paranormal activity, such as the *Amityville Horror* case, flies, bees, and wasps have infested an area where a dark entity resides. Joe and Michael bent down and examined the wasps, discussing this theory for the camera, but also explaining that the wasps could've been there since the previous summer. Then Michael, standing before the camera, interviewed Deb and Tony about the portal.

About that time, a strange feeling overtook Joe. He realized that the investigation now felt totally secular in nature, and he became fearful, not because of the basement itself, but because so many people were now involved who had differing beliefs. He began to wonder if God would lift His protection that Joe felt had been over them.

Joe sidled over to Brad.

"Look at this!" Brad whispered excitedly.

In a picture Brad had taken, Mark strikes an imposing figure in a black leather jacket as he gazes at the camera. And shimmering above

Mark's head is a big, bright orb, almost like a full moon.

"That's unbelievable," Joe said. "I told you this house is haunted, and this is why I wanted to come here and do this investigation. You were worried about getting evidence, but we're going to get more evidence than we can handle."

"I know, you're right," Brad replied, overwhelmed by all he saw. "I'm glad we came."

Later, when Joe digitally enhanced that image, he noticed a human face appeared in it that looked eerily similar to Tony's portrait of Sallie.

Michael wrapped up the on-camera explanation of the portal with Deb and Tony, while Dan remained on the phone.

"While you guys are down there," Dan said when Michael completed his explanation of the portal, "I'm getting almost a burning sensation on my face right now, which is an indicator to me that there's a demonic presence." He later told them that he had a burn on his arm that had appeared when he felt the burning sensation in the basement.

Meanwhile, Michael clambered into the crawlspace with a flashlight and began to search around. Joe hesitated, staring where his friend had disappeared. He then wrinkled his nose against the musty smell, summoned up his courage, and followed Michael. They spent a few minutes examining the walls, using the EMF detector, gauging temperatures with a digital thermometer, and taking digital pictures. They also tried to record digital and analog EVPs, but later findings were negative. Their boots stirred up dust that danced in the flashlight beams.

"I feel like something is watching me," Michael whispered. Joe nodded, trying to ignore the tightness in his chest. He wiped a sweaty palm on his jeans. They brought one of the camera lights into the crawlspace and were getting ready to speak with Dan again when they heard a commotion coming from the basement.

That's where Tony, Deb, Samantha, and Mark were talking while Brad filmed them.

"Boy, this is not a good spot," Tony murmured to Samantha.

"What did you say?" Samantha asked.

"It's just not a good spot," he repeated. "I feel sick to my stomach."

Samantha's jaw dropped open as she looked at his arm. "He's getting cut! He's getting cut!" she blurted out.

Tony showed them his forearm, where a long gash dripped blood on the floor.

"Joe, Michael – Tony's been cut," Brad called out.

Joe and Michael scrambled back out into the main room, hearts pounding, where Tony stood quietly, not seeming surprised. As Brad photographed the cut, drops of blood splattered closer to the black spot on the floor, where the pentagram once existed.

Michael saw the puddle of blood that formed on the floor where Tony stood, and a thought raced through his veins: the nature of what they were dealing with was extremely dangerous for everyone present.

Joe hollered, "Get him away from the pentagram! We don't want the blood to get in there." Then he pushed Tony away from the area. Joe and Mark exchanged a warning look. Because most Satanic rituals have a sacrifice of blood, they believed that if Tony's blood touched the pentagram, it might open a gateway for evil spirits. Joe didn't know if he was falling back on superstition or if it was a reaction to watching too many horror movies, but his first instinct was to stop it.

Mark guided Tony upstairs and cleaned up the cut, and at Dan's urging, the others left the basement as well. "What the heck is happening here?" Michael said.

Deb was overwhelmed, worrying about her husband's attack. "Do we have to keep going on with this?" she asked.

Anna did not say much after seeing Tony's cut, but Joe sensed that their views were different that RIDDIA's. Anna seemed to think that Tony's presence in the house stirred up the spirits, and that's why they attacked him.

Saturday 6 PM

Brad decided to stop work for the day. Joe and Michael thanked Dan for participating in the segment, and asked him to contact them if he sensed that anyone was in danger.

"You guys were telling the truth about this house," Joe said to Deb and Tony. "There is one hundred percent paranormal activity and I feel bad that you didn't get to tell your story before now."

Everyone was dazed by what had happened during the investigation. No one believed they would really see as much activity as they had. They spent a while just discussing the day. They had evidence of three attacks so far, and it seemed that the entity or entities targeted Tony. They had caught orbs on the digital cameras, not just dust orbs but bright lights that they later validated, and they had verified sudden twenty-degree temperature drops in seconds. They had smelled the flower scent on Friday night. Could it all be attributed to having a psychic involved? Could he have been channeling things? Possibly. The point was it had happened.

"I don't know what to do with everything I've seen," Brad said. "I don't know what's going on here, but it isn't phony. I can't debunk it as a hoax."

Joe and Michael were still concerned for Tony's safety. He left and went home, but Deb stayed and visited with them, in case they had more questions for her.

Brad and Samantha were excited about the possibilities for the show, and with what Sunday might bring. "We're just going to gather as much content as we can," Brad said, "and when we get back to Rhode Island, we'll have to sift through everything to see what we'll use."

Their energy was high, and everyone was excited, knowing that the more evidence they obtained, the better for a show. Joe found himself caught up in the whole documentary "fever", forgetting what his mission was. Lots of people had been working on the investigation that day, and Joe and Michael hadn't had a chance to focus on ridding the house of evil spirits.

Brad had arranged a tour of Atchison's famous Hoof and Horn Restaurant, so they headed there. Joe and Michael invited the Pickmans to join them, so Deb went home to pick up Tony and met the others at the restaurant. They toured the restaurant and spoke with the owner and a waitress, and then returned to the Sallie House, without eating dinner.

"Mark didn't accompany us to the restaurant because he didn't have any speaking lines for the documentary," Joe says. "When we returned to the house, Mark was going back and forth with Anna about the Bible and 'knowing the Lord', and what he believed was going on in the house. He was preaching to her, and she was getting a little offended because she felt he was forcing his views upon her. His intentions were good, but he came across strong."

Joe and Michael pulled Mark away from Anna and the tension eased. Joe had ordered pizza and everyone sat around the table and talked about the events of the day. Brad, who had doubted that they would have enough content from the Sallie House alone to make a show, had completely changed his view.

"Now," he said. "With pictures of orbs, Dan's participation, and the attacks on Tony, I wonder what we might have to leave out!"

Saturday 8 PM

The conversation soon died out. It had been another long day; everyone was tired and mentally drained. Deb and Tony left, and RIDDIA and the production crew soon followed, while Greg and Anna again stayed overnight at the Sallie House.

Joe wanted to lie down and go to sleep, but Mark and Michael began to argue. Mark hadn't been aware that a psychic would be involved in the project until Joe actually called Dan on the phone during the filming. Joe didn't intentionally misinform Mark, but Mark was still aggravated about not knowing. He lay on his bed, reading his Bible, and then he jumped up.

"Are you guys nuts?" he exclaimed. "What the heck is going on here? Anna doesn't think *anything* is demonic. You've got a psychic on the phone. What are you doing getting a psychic involved? These people aren't our friends, they just want to make money, they just want a show. We're Christians, and I thought we were supposed to help people and get rid of whatever is in the house. We're supposed to exorcise whatever's there, we're supposed to bless the house, but instead you've got these people involved." He turned to Joe. "We're walking into the line of fire, Joe. The things in the house are going to kill us."

Joe hated to admit it, but Mark was right, he thought.

Mark ranted. "Things are going haywire right now and we haven't done anything about anything yet, as far as praying, spiritual counsel, or anything like that. We're just going with the flow and it isn't right." He hung his head. "We've lost our focus."

"I understand," Michael replied when Mark finished. "But we're trying to do a show. We want to be professional, not come in with guns blazing."

"Who cares if they like us or not?" Mark went on. "Let's do what we came here to do and be done with it."

"Mark's right," Joe said aloud this time. "We have to do something that shows we're different from other teams. If there's something evil, what are we going to do? Get rid of it? Play along? No, it's time to stop being afraid, and do what we came here to do."

The room grew quiet as they reflected on the conversation. Later, as Joe crawled into bed, he knew that they needed to make Sunday's investigation different.

DAY THREE

CHAPTER FIVE

Sunday 8 AM

Joe could hear Brad and Samantha chatting in the dining room as he, Mark, and Michael came downstairs at for breakfast. Snow had fallen overnight, blanketing the ground.

"Well, this is the last day," Brad said. "I'd like to capture more evidence, but I'm happy with what we've achieved so far."

"What are we missing?" Samantha asked.

"We need to film some outdoor shots of the area," Brad continued, "and piece together a closing segment for the documentary."

Joe sat pensively as he ate his waffles, feeling somewhat overwhelmed. Everything that led him to this point seemed to have paid off, all the hard work setting things up for their visit. But he was still questioning his motives. Was this documentary more about financial gain? His passion for what God had called him to do had become clouded.

As everyone finished breakfast, the discussion centered on the last few of odds and ends they needed to accomplish. They planned where to film Michael and Joe's wrap-up interviews about the weekend. No cue cards, just their truthful opinions.

"Whatever you're going to do that makes you different from other teams," Brad said. "You only have today to do it."

They were all tired and burned out mentally, and the drive to get started eluded them. Brad said if they finished everything at a decent time, he would take everyone out to dinner, where they could watch the AFC Championship between the New England Patriots and Indianapolis Colts.

First on the agenda was a visit to the Pickmans, who had invited Joe, Michael, and the camera crew over to their house at eleven. When they arrived, Tony presented them with homemade pies and banana bread to take home with them.

As they talked, Tony made a rather startling observation about the previous couple of days. "I know the group was wondering why I didn't get excited about being scratched," he said. "I don't seem bothered too much by this, but I've been dealing with this for thirteen years, if not longer. I've just gotten used to it. Half the time I don't know it's happening. Someone has to point it out to me. I don't feel anything, except maybe a little cold."

Deb spoke up, hesitantly. "We've been dealing with something dark in the Sallie House."

Joe was a little surprised. "You've never said that to me before," he said.

"I know. I've been too scared to acknowledge what may be in the house."

While they conversed, Joe kept thinking that this was why his group was in Kansas, to help them, to offer them hope that what's in the house can be stopped and they won't have to deal with it anymore. Deb and Tony knew RIDDIA's approach was a Christian one, and Joe realized that they might not share his religious beliefs. But as Deb had talked about the spirits being "demonic", and not just dark, as she had acknowledged the possibility of evil, he realized that perhaps the Pickmans were believers and were receptive to Christianity, so Joe felt that he could now approach the situation through prayer.

As Joe and Michael concluded the conversation with the Pickmans,

Joe's cell phone rang. Dan Hernandez was calling from San Diego, saying he was again feeling a strong presence in the Sallie House. No one knew how accurate Dan's assessment was, so they decided to go back to the house right then. Dan also told them that he had stayed up Saturday evening into Sunday morning to see if he sensed any danger on the group's behalf. If he had felt the presence in the Sallie House follow them to the Glick Mansion, he was going to warn them. Joe didn't really know what to make of Dan's reasoning for staying up, but Dan's concern touched him.

Sunday 2 PM

They arrived at the Sallie House around two o'clock, and the house was empty. Greg had left for home earlier in the day, and Anna from MPRS was not there. The quiet assailed them. Even though the heating was on, Joe noticed a distinct chill in the living room. An eerie, unsettled feeling washed over him, something more than just the emptiness of the house. Meanwhile, Mark came over from the Glick Mansion and everyone readied themselves for more filming. Despite Joe's initial sense of unease, neither he nor Michael felt the particular presence that Dan had described.

Joe called Dan and put him on speakerphone, and Dan directed them to the smaller bedroom upstairs. Once there, they used the digital thermometer to measure the temperature and noticed a quick drop of fifteen degrees. As they stood there, they began to smell lilacs, gardenias, and then a foul stench, like rotten eggs.

"Whoa, that's awful," Samantha said, waving a hand in front of her nose.

"That kind of foul odor typically permeates an area when a demon is present," Joe said, growing more guarded.

Brad looked around warily.

Michael couldn't help but think of what Anna said about the home. In that bedroom, Michael understood when she called the house a supernatural bus stop for spirits. It felt to him like multiple spirits plagued the home at the same time.

Dan instructed them once again to pray the Lord's Prayer. They recited it once, and Dan asked them to repeat it, and as they did the second time, the room filled with warmth.

"I can feel the presence has moved, so the prayer worked, but I think using the Lord's name has aggravated it," Dan said. As on Saturday, he then claimed the entity had moved to the basement, but he urged them not to go down there again.

As Dan talked, Michael looked disgusted, and Joe could tell he was annoyed. Joe felt the same way. He knew he had hesitated Saturday to "do things the right way" mostly because Brad and Samantha seemed so pleased with how the investigation was going without anyone interjecting "religion" into it. Since they had financed the trip, Joe figured he should respect their wishes. And because there were so many other things happening and so many other people around, he was also intimidated to speak up about their Christian mission. But now Joe wondered if perhaps he and Michael still had an opportunity to perform a blessing on the house.

"Let's go do what we came here to do," Michael said, and raced downstairs. Everyone marched after him.

Joe's eyes darted around the room, at the dark corners and the black opening to the crawlspace. Chills raced up and down his spine. "Was this thing going to finally manifest itself?" he thought. The rotten odor from upstairs was gone, replaced with flowery smells and a warm feeling. "Was it deceiving them, setting them up, only to trap them down here?"

Michael led the way in the crawlspace, with Joe right behind, while Dan remained on the phone. Mark, Tony, and Deb stayed in the main part of the basement, while Brad and Samantha crowded into the entrance as the camcorder and movie camera filmed the scene, its bright light illuminating the area.

The temperature abruptly plummeted and they knew something was down there with them.

"I could feel it," Joe recalled. "Then Dan said the entity was in the crawlspace with us. Once again, things I would sense and feel but I didn't say aloud, Dan would mention as well. I knew there was something to the gift he claimed to have."

As the presence intensified, Michael noticed a mist forming in the corner. He shone the flashlight on it as Brad moved into the crawlspace and shot some pictures.

"Oh my gosh, I can see it!" he exclaimed.

Joe saw it as well, shimmering in the light. He and Michael didn't know whether it was a spray from one of the pipes leaking or spirit manifestation, but they were disturbed all the same. Later, upon closer examination, one picture showed beams of light filtering downward with orbs in the rays, "almost like a release of spirits rising through the portal," Joe says.

Joe wondered if the mist would form into an actual demonic apparition. So he did the only thing he could think to do – pray. He closed his eyes and began to pray in the Spirit and ask God to send His angels to protect them.

"You are not welcome here," Michael said to the entity. "I am sick of you scaring people." He continued as if talking to it.

When Mark heard Joe praying, he rushed into the crawlspace and stood back-to-back with Joe, two soldiers covering each other in battle, and prayed with Joe. A few seconds later, Tony and Deb edged into the crawlspace with them.

Dan encouraged them to continue praying. Michael blessed the home, "I bless this house in the name of Jesus. I command anything that's in here to leave this house, and to leave the Pickmans alone. You have no power here." The chill increased. Michael chanted prayers from the *Roman Ritual*, as well. "I cast you out, unclean spirit, from this place."

Joe closed his eyes and stood in a trance, continuing in deep prayer, trusting through faith that he wouldn't be hurt.

They prayed and prayed as the minutes flew by. "I feel it getting weaker," Dan said.

The film camera kept rolling, and Brad snapped more pictures.

"Finish it off," Dan encouraged them.

"I bind you in the name of Jesus," Joe said. "Leave this house and never return."

Within seconds warmth filled the area, and a sense of total peace washed over Joe. Then Dan spoke. "I feel it's gone," Dan said. Everyone cheered.

Joe knew the presence of God was with them. Michael found himself under demonic oppression during the blessing, a feeling that to this day makes him uncomfortable to describe. They had been there for over an hour and, finally, the home had been purged of the evil intelligence dwelling in it.

Sunday 4 PM

They moved back to the main part of the basement, where they stood around, hugging and shaking hands. Brad began to cry, but he couldn't explain why. Joe believed it was the hand of God on Brad.

After a few minutes, they all regained their composure. Joe was ecstatic, and he knew this was an experience he would never forget. Even Brad and Samantha had big grins on their faces. Joe and Michael thanked Dan and ended the call. Brad spent a few minutes working to set up the final wrap-up scene. Joe and Michael stood at the top of the stairs looking down into the camera.

After sharing their conclusions that demons had indeed manifested themselves in the house, Joe and Michael ended the documentary:

Joe: "We want to thank you for being a part of this investigation."

Michael: "We hope that the information was helpful and informative."

Joe: "We are here to validate…"

Michael: "educate…"

Joe: "and authenticate…"

Michael: "the supernatural world."

Both: "Until next time…"

Joe: "I'm Joe Cetrone…"

Michael: "I'm Michael Piccerelli…"

Both: "Have a great night."

EPILOGUE

It wasn't until two days later, after returning home, that Joe had time to reflect on the weekend. As he lay in bed in complete darkness and silence, Joe began replaying every scene of the past weekend in his mind. Though it had been fun and adventurous, he felt strange, now that it was over and they were all back to their own lives, wondering if they done the right thing? What if their lives were never the same, or what if nothing became of the investigation? He was overwhelmed with fear, excitement, and dread. He knew that he'd lost his focus and that he had allowed too many people to dictate the course of the weekend. He knew he hadn't stayed true to his mission. And he surmised that, because they had not honored God in their work, God would not honor what they had done. After so much soul-searching, Joe came to believe that RIDDIA had had no business going to the Sallie House in the first place. Truth be told, their adventure had been more for profit and gain than anything else. "The sad part was, even before we started looking at the footage and bringing the show to life, I knew it was already over."

+   +   +

Was Joe's assessment accurate? Did God withhold His blessing of the project because Joe hadn't taken charge of the investigation? Joe, Michael, and Mark believed that they had been successful in ridding the

71

Sallie House of demonic infestation, and the production crew had lots of good footage for a documentary. What could be missing?

But over time, things began to unravel for those involved in the investigation. Soon after they returned from Kansas, RIDDIA disbanded. Michael faced financial difficulties. And the documentary has yet to be sold to any network.

And were their lives the same after the investigation? The simple answer to that is "no". But nothing is ever as straightforward as that.

Once they returned to Rhode Island, Brad, Samantha, Joe, and Michael spent almost seventy hours editing film footage just to create a trailer for the documentary. They sifted through the raw footage and chose some of the best scenes. Brad added music to scenes, and he also had Joe and Michael do some voice-overs for the sequences. As the week progressed, Joe and Michael watched in awe as the trailer came to life. Once completed, Joe, Michael, and Samantha viewed the final product. They all agreed Brad had done an incredible job and that the trailer depicted most of the salient points of the investigation, most notably the attacks on Tony.

Watching it, however, Joe realized one other thing. "Brad removed anything that had to do with Christianity. All the prayer sequences, the last encounter in the basement with the mist, were not there. The religious focus was the most important aspect, and he cut it all out."

But Brad didn't want 'religion' in the documentary. He didn't think it would help sell the piece, so he made no changes to it. He and Samantha shopped the trailer around to agents and industry representatives who might be interested. In the end, nobody liked it, saying that nothing set this show idea apart from any other show on the subject. Brad conceded that they may have missed the mark, as shows about the paranormal had flooded the industry.

"What's frustrating," Joe says, "Is that almost eighteen months later, I saw a show that incorporated the Bible in a paranormal investigation, similar to what we had done. I was so angry I called Brad at eleven-thirty and yelled at him for taking those scenes out of the trailer. He had been watching the same show and he agreed with me, saying he'd 'dropped the ball' on that."

And unfortunately, as has happened to other investigators who entered the Sallie House, something about the house affected the members of RIDDIA long after they left it. Each struggled with different challenges. Not only had RIDDIA discontinued investigations, but Joe and Michael ceased broadcasting their radio show *Strange Encounters*.

"Is it possible that some entity or entities from the Sallie House followed us home?" Joe says. "Maybe. When we were at the airport in Kansas, waiting for our flight home, I found out that Michael had taken dirt and some plastic toy letters from the children's bedroom, and I've wondered if bringing items from the house had any negative spiritual affects on us. I have no way to prove anything, but I still question it."

Deb and Tony Pickman, having dealt with adversity surrounding the Sallie House for almost sixteen years, tried to regain a normal life after their weekend with RIDDIA. They believe that RIDDIA's investigation and solid attempts to bind the evil that infested the Sallie House was a prelude to what they encountered later. They still had periodic visits to the Sallie House after that January weekend and other investigative teams reported negative trauma after being in the home. Although skeptical at first of these claims, the Pickmans now believe in the house's far-reaching effects. They remain intrigued with the paranormal and the Sallie House, and have decided to write a book about their experiences while living there.

Since she worked on Joe and Michael's radio show *Strange Encounters*, Dawn Pierce spoke with Joe and Michael regularly. But she noticed the aftereffects of the Sallie House, even though she didn't venture to Kansas with Joe and Michael. With the demise of *Strange Encounters*, Dawn spoke with them less frequently, and then not at all. The paranormal nightmare involving her son Jordyn continued, becoming so disturbing that Dawn finally moved her family out of Massachusetts.

Todd Bates, who had introduced Joe and Michael to the Sallie

House, observed a difference in his psyche after RIDDIA's investigation, what he describes as a 'spiritual lifting'. However, he also expressed concern that he was under attack by unseen forces after his involvement with the Sallie House. He wrestled with depression, took a break from working in the paranormal world, and almost lost his radio show.

Mark Brown endured some traumatic events as well. Within two years of the investigation, he lost a great job, a girlfriend, his faith, and, for a time, his home. For months after returning from Kansas, he would hear footsteps walking on his bed at night. He called Joe in the middle of the night because he was afraid to sleep. However, at the time of this writing, Mark is on a positive path. He has reconnected with his faith and teaches at his church.

Michael Piccerelli suffered through terrible depression after the investigation. A recovering alcoholic and addict, he began drinking and using drugs again, which caused his girlfriend to leave him. He eventually checked himself into a clinic in Florida. Now, two years later, he is much healthier. He is clean and sober, has a good job, a new girlfriend, and has maintained his faith in God.

Joe fell away from the vision he believed God had for him, to teach and educate about the paranormal as it relates to the Bible. For no apparent reason, he stopped talking to everybody involved with the case. Like others, he struggled in his marriage and lost his job. He felt under attack psychologically as well, battled depression and anxiety, feared death, and doubted the Bible and all that he knew to be true.

Over time, Joe worked through these issues. His marriage became stronger, and he is again attending church, where he plays drums in a worship team. He is spiritually grounded again and has used his investigative experiences, and the lessons he's learned from studying the paranormal, to start a ministry educates people about the dangers of demonic forces that lurk in the supernatural realm. He decided to write about the Sallie House investigation because he felt the need to tell the story from his perspective, bringing closure to the events of that weekend in January, 2007.

But questions remain about the Sallie House and Atchison, Kansas.

"I can only speak for myself," Joe says. "But I can attest to paranormal activity in the Sallie House. We captured pictures of spirit orbs with identifiable facial features. In digital pictures, spinning orbs, grayish type smudges or blurs, hovered around us. On a few occasions we felt cold spot areas with a twenty-degree drop in temperature in a matter of seconds. I witnessed a man being physically attacked on three separate occasions right in front of my eyes. We made continuous attempts to debunk all of this, but we couldn't. I believe that our trip to the Sallie House proved that there is life after death."

Although Joe believed that the investigation was successful, he wasn't able to convince others to leave the house alone. And he wonders if having psychics and investigators coming into the house and contacting spirits since RIDDIA's visit has again opened the house to demonic activity.

What *is* the presence residing in the home: an angry, demonic spirit, or a benign, protective spirit and nothing more? Is the home is a gateway to another dimension?

"As a Christian, I didn't believe this," Joe says. "I was always taught human spirits cannot come back, they either go to heaven or hell. But this experience confused me at times, because I wondered if what I learned was correct. I believe if God wants to show us a human spirit, He can, but I'm just not sure what to make of everything I saw at the Sallie House."

"Dan Hernandez's observations also baffled me. I always believed 'psychics' or 'sensitives' were either fakes or they were receiving their messages from the demonic realm because that's what the Bible teaches. Though I believe that to be true in a lot ways, it didn't seem to be the case with Dan. What confused me is that he endorsed use of the Lord's Prayer, and in fact, he prayed with us. In the end, we validated that his gift was not fake because he knew things that nobody could know unless they were there themselves."

No matter one's beliefs, it is a fact that strange occurrences frequently take place at the Sallie House. Joe speculates that Tony Pickman was a catalyst for what lies in the home, and that is why so much activity has been reported only after the Pickmans first lived in the house. And as more and more people go into the home, dabbling in séances, Tarot cards, and Ouija boards, they may be opening a doorway that isn't meant to be opened. Joe also wonders if the spiritual activity, not only in the Sallie House but in Atchison, can be traced to possible Satanic practices taking place back in the 1800's, especially at the Gargoyle Mansion. And does the town's own promotion of its haunted reputation feed the spiritual activity? Joe thinks this could be the case.

"To speak of the Sallie House being haunted by human or demonic spirits is left up for interpretation because they both exist," Joe says. "I personally believe the entity or entities were demonic. What lies in the home and around Atchison could be anything you want it to be, almost like a 'familiar' or 'shape-shifting' spirit. But the Bible cautions against 'familiar spirits', a demon that can take the form of a human in order to deceive. Also, demons will engage in activities in threes, mocking the Trinity, and the entities in the house attacked Tony three times during the weekend. All that, plus how the spirits reacted when we performed the blessing that last day in the basement was further validation that we were dealing with demonic entities. But even if we were to address this on a non-Biblical level, whatever is in that home and surrounding area is dark in nature, and should be avoided."

Finis

Please visit our websites for:

- Study guide questions for your reading group or Bible study
- Deleted scenes from <u>The Sallie House</u>
- Scripture references about spirits
- Pictures taken during the Sallie House investigation, including orbs
- Information about our other books

www.reneepawlish.com
www.spiritfire7.com

ABOUT THE AUTHORS

Renée Pawlish is the author of <u>Nephilim Genesis of Evil</u>. She resides in Littleton, CO.

Joe Cetrone is the author of two books, <u>The Invisible War</u> and <u>God, the Bible, and the Afterlife</u>, and is a teacher on spiritual warfare and paranormal phenomena. He resides in Westerly, Rhode Island.